Prea
TWO
VOICES

Sermons on the Women
in Jesus' Life

Preaching in TWO VOICES

Sermons on the Women in Jesus' Life

William D. Watley
Suzan D. Johnson Cook

Judson Press ® Valley Forge

Library of Congress Cataloging-in-Publication Data

Cook, Suzan D. Johnson
　　Preaching in two voices : sermons of the women in Jesus' life/
Suzan D. Johnson Cook, William D. Watley.
　　　　p.　　cm.
　　Includes bibliographical references.
　　ISBN 0-8170-1173-0
　　1. Jesus Christ—Friends and associates—Sermons. 2. Jesus
Christ—Views on women—Sermons. 3. Women in the Bible.
4. Sermons, American—Afro-American authors. 5. Sermons,
American—Women authors. I. Watley, William D. II. Title.
BT590.W6J64　　　　1992
225.9'22—dc20　　　　　　　　　　　　　　　　91-38770
[B]　　　　　　　　　　　　　　　　　　　　　　　　CIP

Preface

I was raised in a very stable and secure home, with nurturing parents who sought to prepare their children for the "real world." Certainly my brother and I had the normal household chores, as both our parents worked. Yet these duties and responsibilities were shared by all, not divided along gender lines. We were a family, so everyone contributed. The heroes and heroines and leaders discussed in our home were both men and women. It was, I felt, a normal environment. We took these healthy and balanced attitudes with us the rest of our lives. I genuinely felt that both women and men could be contributors to all segments of society.

It was only after entering seminary at the age of twenty-three that I began to find that there was a "gender issue." As I wrestled with the various questions raised in our classes and in my private study, I also served as a student minister in an African American church so that my culture would be affirmed as I went through this new and shocking growth process. As I began to observe, learn from, and participate in the traditional church structure, the overpowering oppression of women became most evident. I recognized that not only was I considered inferior because I was a female but also that in many instances females were nonentities, both in the practical and historical interpretations. Biblical Scripture, translated by men, often did not include "my" story. Sermons by leading preachers, with the exception of ones on Women's Day, usually focused on men. Yet, I believed God called me to preach the unadulterated gospel of Jesus Christ, and I persevered.

In my last semester of seminary, I was called to serve as interim pastor and in the same year full-time minister of the historic Mariners' Temple Baptist Church, the oldest Baptist church in Manhattan. I succeeded twenty-five men who had served in this place, and, as history would have it, also ushered in a new era for women, especially African American women, as senior pastors in American Baptist churches. Through this experience several doors have been opened, some just ajar, while others still remain closed. Yet one of the most affirming experiences was my participation in a unique doctoral program at United Theological Seminary in Dayton, Ohio, as a Sam Proctor Fellow. As one of two entering females, and the only female graduate out of this class of sixteen, the journey was a stimulating one, for I was able to sit and dialogue with men who genuinely became my brothers, colleagues, and friends as we began to raise concerns for the African American church in the twenty-first century. But it also provided opportunity for me to share and even vent my struggles and journey as a pastor who was female.

As the pain in many cases surfaced, I read, prayed about, listened to, and even attacked the patriarchal system that had been created and which often denied me entry and access. As I began to review and analyze the hundreds of sermons delivered, I began to notice that three-fourths of my sermons focused on women in the New Testament. I was hungry for the "living bread," and I needed to know about sisters and their faith journeys; I was identifying with them in a strong way.

During this period of my doctoral studies, two things also happened. First, Dr. William Watley, my co-author, and I began to raise the same concerns about the exclusion of women in writings and ecclesiastical circles, while also affirming the importance of their contributions. We, through the Holy Spirit, agreed it was time to highlight some of the women in Jesus' ministry. We were both teaching seminary classes in which more than 50 percent of the students were female; we were both pastors who understood that 75 percent of our traditional churches are female congregants; and we wanted the current and next generation to know the "whole story." Therefore, in this compilation of sermons, you will find our sensitive, moving, and sometimes even angry interpretations of the women in Jesus' life that we hope will "trouble the waters" and also be good news to those in captivity.

This book, then, is an exciting experiment between two African American pastors—one male, one female—who love and are concerned about women and men in the church. As you read our sermons from our own perspectives and certainly from the traditions that have shaped us, you will be introduced to eight women who lived with, moved with, and served with Jesus. It is our prayer that Jesus will live and move in you as you read this work.

The second thing that happened during my doctoral studies was that I met Dr. Otis Moss, the renowned pastor of the Mount Olivet Baptist Church in Cleveland, Ohio, who listened sometimes for hours to my frustration as a woman in this time in history, and who is committed to justice on all fronts. He suggested that I invite Dr. Ella Mitchell, who presently team teaches with her husband, Henry, at the Interdenominational Theological Center in Atlanta, to have a round table with other women clergy to see how she "survived" those forty-plus years before we newcomers were on the scene and how she managed to do it with such a "gentle strength."

Recently I followed through on his suggestion. Dr. Mitchell came to Mariners', and sixteen women clergy, four of whom are now my "daughters in ministry," joined her for lunch. We sat at her feet and listened to her wisdom. Many of us cried. We all prayed. But one thing was clear when we left the table. There is hope, even when things seem hopeless. There are times to "move," yet we don't always need to push, for God has already prepared the way for our ministries.

It is my prayer and hope that this book will, via the movement of the Holy Spirit, push us all into a sensitized spirit of inclusivity, where, as did Jesus, we can join and say, "Whosoever will, let her come."

My thanks and gratitude go to the Johnson family, who taught me to be all I desire to be, who affirm my calling and gifts, and who support my ministry; to the wonderful congregation of Mariners' Temple Baptist Church, who allow me to be their pastor and to develop these gifts and discover untapped ones; to my five daughters in ministry: Sheila, Henrietta, Gladys, Carolyn, and Valerie, for whom I hope their journey and future will be a little easier and a lot more human; and to all the women whose lives I've touched and who have touched mine.

Suzan D. Johnson Cook
January 1991

To grow up male in America is in many ways to grow up a chauvinist. A number of us males do not intend to emerge as chauvinists, any more than persons intend to become racists or bigots. We do not adopt chauvinism as a distinct philosophy, ideology, or theology for our lives. We just acquire certain perceptions and attitudes about women that we receive through education, custom, religion, and language and that we accept as normative and right. Therefore, if one is male, one has to unlearn much of what one has learned regarding womanhood. One has to learn new ways of thinking and interpretation which translate into orthopraxy.

I am grateful to all of the women who have helped me come to a more profound understanding of what it means to be female, African American, and Christian. I am grateful to my grandmother, Mrs. Fannie Thomas, of sacred memory, who was a paradigm of strength and independence. I am grateful to my mother, Mrs. Marian Watley, for her prayerful counsel and exemplary life. I am grateful to my wife of twenty-two years, Muriel, who faithfully and patiently loves and labors with me. I am grateful to my sister and friend, Mrs. Carolyn Scavella, not only for her usual assistance in the preparation of this manuscript, but also for her insights which have been a significant part of my growth.

I am grateful to my daughter, Jennifer, who constantly challenges her father to think new thoughts. **This book is dedicated to my daughter, Jennifer Elaine,** my firstborn, with the hope that she will spend her adult womanhood in a freer world and in a more enabling church.

I would also like to thank my former administrative assistant, Mr. Vaughn Jackson, and my present administrative assistant, Mrs. Constance Wright, for their painstaking typing of this manuscript. I am grateful to the members of the St. James AME Church family, particularly the women of the church who are living examples of what it means to be female, African American, and Christian.

I am indeed grateful for the privilege of having as colleague, friend, sister in the faith, and co-author, Rev. Suzan D. Johnson Cook.

William D. Watley
January 1991

CONTENTS

1

Anna:
It's Worth the Wait!

Luke 2:36–38
Suzan D. Johnson Cook

And there was one Anna, a prophetess, the daughter of Phan-uel, of the tribe of Aser: she was of a great age, and had lived with an husband seven years from her virginity; And she was a widow of about fourscore and four years, which departed not from the temple, but served God with fastings and prayers night and day. And she coming in that instant gave thanks likewise unto the Lord, and spake of him to all them that looked for redemption in Jerusalem (Luke 2:36 – 38, KJV).

When Jesus was born, many powerful things began to happen. The Word was being made flesh, just as God had said; prophecy was being fulfilled, and many played a part in the enactment of God being revealed and made known to the people of God. The old was being passed away and the new was at hand; yet there were still some old customs that were being held onto. The Law of Moses was the dominant traditional expression of faith followed by the Jewish people, and as was the custom, Mary and Joseph, Jesus' earthly parents, were preparing to make their sacrifice of thanksgiving unto God for the healthy birth of their firstborn son, who had been so miraculously conceived, delivered, and even named. Being poor, they were not expected to give more than a pair of turtledoves or two young pigeons, which were to be offered at the altar in the temple eight days after the circumcision. As they were preparing to follow this Mosaic custom, they encountered two persons who were waiting at the temple. The first was a devout man named Simeon whose only desire in life was to wait to hold this God child in his arms and bless him. As he did this, he confirmed what

1

the Spirit had already affirmed in him—that indeed this Christ child would cause the Gentiles to have a light and the glory of the Lord to be revealed. The testimony that is recorded about Simeon was that the Holy Spirit was upon him, for he also knew that the rising and falling of many in Israel would occur as a result of the sign that the Lord had already given. Wouldn't it be wonderful if as others wrote our life stories, they would say the Holy Spirit was upon us?

After Simeon's prophetic utterance and the fulfillment of his desire to see this child, we are introduced to a powerful woman, a prophetess named Anna, who also had been waiting for the coming of the Messiah.

Anna was about eighty-four years old, a woman who lived in times when societal pressures dictated that a woman's self-worth was often determined by the man or men she had in her life. But Anna apparently lived alone. She was a widow whose husband had died only seven years after their marriage, and who by all indications had pledged her remaining days to the service of the Lord. Here she was, a widow from the tribe of Asher (Aser), one of the lost tribes of Israel. Not much is known about her heritage other than her father's first name, Phanuel. She had none of those things that many women in her age group might have had: children, grandchildren, remembrances of family reunions. She only had a desire to see and serve the Lord. She was a woman in the midst of a world that would by most standards reject her. Yet she found solace for her soul; she found contentment in being where the Lord was. And after Simeon was able to bless the child, according to the time and will of God, she, too, had an opportunity to make her own expression of thanksgiving and blessings to God for the gift of this child to Jerusalem and to the world.

She had a special spiritual calling upon her life and was interested in those who looked for redemption. Because of her calling and her seriousness about her mission, she stayed at the temple both night and day, with both fasting and prayer. In fact, it is purported that she had her own room at the temple because of her constant presence there. And when Jesus' parents and Simeon were there, she, too, gave thanks unto the Lord.

This is such a simple yet profound story about the faithfulness of one woman who, despite the odds, had her focus and her mission clearly centered. As the opportunity arose to be a vessel for God, she was not only in the right place at the right time, but also in the right spirit for God to be able to use her in the way that was necessary before the parents could continue their pilgrimage back to Galilee, to their own city of Nazareth.

This text raises some questions for those of us who are or who know women facing both times and challenges that by all surface indications are closed doors to our opportunities. But I have learned that in God there are times and places beneath the surface that allow us to realize that our difficulties become God's opportunities. Despite the odds, despite the societal pressures of being widowed young and not being encouraged or able to remarry and being from one of the tribes that was lost, Anna found the courage and fortitude to find a place where she could be used and be a blessing for the kingdom; she also found a positive identity in Christ.

As an African American woman, I see certain parallels between Anna's story and my own. First, there is uncertainty about the tribal background of my ancestors. Second, there is the continuing pressure to be married and connected with a man. My peers do not understand what it means for a woman to spend so much time at the temple in prayer and devotional life. And, like Anna, I've had to learn to wait my turn, often waiting until after the men have had a chance to make their expressions to Jesus.

Yet this story is a clear reminder that no matter when the opportunity arises, we need to be ready to seize the moment. Anna was a New Testament Deborah, a woman who was waiting for *her* time when all the rest of Israel was experiencing a paralysis of fear. But, Deborah, like Anna, rose to the occasion and was able to lead Israel to victory in God's time and according to God's will. Anna was able to deal seriously with the fact that first the temple was there for her, a place where she could find rest for her soul, a refuge in the time of trouble. The nation of Israel was in trouble; political authorities and others were closing in on anyone who professed belief in the coming Son of God and the Son of man. Yet Anna could go to the temple and make contact with the one who had promised the Redeemer would come.

Prophetic voices before her had already told her both his name and his chosen responsibility. Isaiah said it best in chapter 9, verse 6:

For to us a child is born,
to us a Son is given;
and the government will be upon his shoulder,
and his name will be called
"Wonderful Counselor, Mighty God,
Everlasting Father, Prince of Peace."

And now she would be able to hold the one in her arms who would have the very government upon his shoulders. Therefore, the temple was central to helping her focus in her waiting time, to be reminded of the prophetic voices that preceded her own.

Lately, as the pace of life becomes more and more frenetic for modern-day prophets and prophetesses, I find myself going more often to a temple. I find myself so tired from what I have done for others who have come to the temple that many times I have neglected to be somewhere just waiting for the Promised One. Last month, after conducting a Sunday morning service in my own church, I went to the nave of the historic Riverside Church. I just needed to be alone with God, where there were neither demands nor expectations, but where, as did Anna, I could be still enough and ready enough to receive Christ whenever and however he chose to come to me. The calm I felt in being in Christ's presence must have been close to the emotional feeling Anna experienced when she knew that the One for whom she had been waiting was now in her midst.

But there was something else special about Anna's being there on that day that was special to Jesus and both his parents. She was prepared; that is, she was "prayed up." My ancestors from my own lost tribes used to sing, "I woke up this morning with my mind stayed on Jesus," testifying to the fact that they had prayed all night long. Prayer is the foundation of each of our ministries, both lay and ordained. Prayer allows us to be able to recognize with a discerning spirit when it is God coming to us and not someone or something else. Anna had prayed before Jesus arrived; in fact, her devotional life was so intact that often she accompanied her prayer with fasting, denying herself the physical and material so that more emphasis could be placed on the spiritual. When one learns how to pray, one has the opportunity to get more mileage out of the journey, for prayer centers; prayer settles; prayer calms. Perhaps that is why Isaiah said, "Thou wilt keep him [her] in perfect peace, whose mind is stayed on thee, because he [she] trusteth in thee" (Isaiah 26:3).

There are days when no one else understands what I seem to understand nor sees the vision I see. Often it can be a frustrating experience. I want the ministry to move in a certain way by a certain time because I am sure that the potential is there and because God has given me the certainty and assurance that it is God's will for my congregation. Yet many cannot and do not see it. It is in these moments that I have especially learned how to pray. And I, too, have found what is meant by "perfect peace." Perfect peace often means waiting, even when others do not understand why you are waiting. I am sure that Anna's activity and the intensity of it were not popular. Yet it is in the middle of the unpopular that one must make a faith step and learn how to make the faith decisions that will be best for one's own soul and well-being. Anna exhibited this kind of faith and took a risk to be where she felt God would have her to be.

Even beyond being prayed up, beyond the discipline in fasting, and beyond being at the temple, the place of worship, Anna's witness gives us still more. When Jesus arrived, she knew him and took him in her arms. In other words, she received him willingly. When Jesus is ready to enter our lives, we, too, must be ready to receive him. How often do we miss the opportunity to be blessed even beyond the measure of our own expectation? Anna knew that he was coming, but she did not know that she would be able to have these precious moments alone with him. Hundreds of young men and women come into our ministry each week, many of whom have heard about Jesus, but many of these young people really know little about experiencing him personally. Because God is God, they have the opportunity to receive Jesus and to hold onto him.

I believe one of the most important lessons for us from this sister's story is that she was there in partnership with Simeon. He was not alone in waiting for and in receiving the Lord; she was there too. As we move toward a new millennium, we will have to realize that women will play a significant role in the kingdom of God.

Just as Anna caught the attention of this Gospel writer, there are women today who are capturing the attention of those who understand the prophetic significance of this new time and place in history. Men who traditionally filled the temples and who were waiting for the coming of the Lord are now realizing that many of those who are praying alongside them, and often praying at the temple before and after them, are women who are necessary partners in the advancement of the worship and devotional life of today's church. There are women who have been waiting to become empowered in preaching, and, like Anna, they will preach redemption to God's people. Truly, sons and daughters, as Joel envisioned, are prophesying what God has given to them as instruments of change in this ever-changing era.

As the walls of Berlin have come down; as the Germans have reunited; as South African prisons are releasing political prisoners, and the ugly walls of apartheid are beginning to crumble; as the Namibians become free and independent; and as forms of new expression for African Americans rise to the forefront in our own nation, God needs prophetic voices in times that may appear to be pathetic. In each of these scenarios, women are playing critical roles as they walk beside men. As children, we learned to sing many songs of our rich African American heritage. One of these was: "Walk together, children. Don't you get weary. There's a great camp-meeting in the Promised Land." This reminds us as a people of faith and color that the struggles that face and await us affect all of us, and if we work for change together, then we can celebrate together when we all reach the "promised land."

Anna, along with Simeon, waited for the promise of the Father—the promise that Jesus would come. They received what they had been waiting for; but more than that, they received *more* than they had hoped for. Anna paved the way for sisters such as myself, that we may be reminded to hold on, even when others may not understand. If we are faithful and true to our calling, then truly God may use us, too, in these temples where we are.

2

Anna:
Great Expectations

(A New Year Sermon)

Luke: 2:36–38
William D. Watley

When I was a small boy, one of my favorite snacks or items of junk food was a box of caramel-covered popcorn known as Cracker Jacks. Having had a sweet tooth since my earliest recollection, I naturally preferred caramel popcorn over regular popcorn. Just any caramel popcorn, however, would not suffice for me—I always preferred Cracker Jacks. As I look back upon these years, I have come to understand that my preference for this brand was not simply because of its taste or the peanuts that were mixed in with the popcorn, but because each box contained a surprise gift or trinket. These small trinkets were, for the most part, cheap little plastic toys or paper items that broke or tore easily. After all, one can only expect so much from a toy that comes out of a box of popcorn. However, as a child, my delight was in eating or sifting through the box of Cracker Jacks until I found my surprise gift; there was always a sense of anticipation, expectancy, and mystery. Whenever I found my prize, I held it with joy, as if I had made some great discovery or found some valued treasure.

One of the characteristics of childhood that we too easily lose, that would put some vitality and excitement into some of our dull personalities and monotonous lives and routines, is the sense of great expectations. Today as we stand at the beginning of a New Year, do we have great expectations? As we work our way through the days ahead, will we be looking for any surprises to delight us?

7

We stand at the beginning of this year carrying some baggage from the past. We did not solve all of our problems from last year; consequently, we know that some of the same issues and people that we wrestled with last year will have to be contended with this year. We know that this year will hold its share of mountains to be climbed and challenges to be met. But do we also have any hopes or dreams for this new year? Are we bold enough to look for something in this year other than trouble and anticipate something besides problems?

We've all heard the old blues saying that "I been down so long that down looks like it's up." The trouble with too many of us is that we've been in the rut we're in for so long that we have ceased trying to get out. We have accepted our lot as definitive and have assumed that things will not or cannot be any better. For some of us every day is the same, every week is the same, every year is the same, everybody we meet is the same, every preacher we hear is the same, every doctor we visit is the same, every teacher we meet is the same, every church we attend is the same. Nothing ever changes for some of us. We just go on subsisting and surviving and moving on as best we can from year to year, grade to grade, preacher to preacher, relationship to relationship—without any great expectations to put life into our tired souls, smiles on our bland and blank faces, interest into our dull conversations, and excitement into our monotonous routines.

Today we are challenged to believe and look for something good in the box that we are holding. We are challenged to have some great expectations for this coming year. I know that this may be a departure for a number of us because some of us are not content unless we are begging and complaining, whining and crying. There are some people who specialize in seeing the negative, who are never content, and who can always find something to criticize or complain about.

As we stand at the beginning of another year, we are challenged in the name of the God who gives us a brand new day every day—one that we have never seen before and one that we shall never see again—to have some great expectations. We are challenged in the name of the God who every spring brings new grass up out of the ground and new flowers into bloom, who covers the branches of the trees with new leaves and awakens hibernating animals to face a new season, to have some great expectations. We are challenged in the name of a God who still hangs in the heavens a rainbow that is made from the particles of the storm, who talks about a new covenant and a new baptism, and who has said, "Behold, I make all things new" (Revelation 21:5), to have some great expectations. We are challenged in the name of this great God to believe that life holds some good things for us.

If the manufacturer of Cracker Jacks is able to put some small trinkets in the boxes for the enjoyment of those who purchase that product, then our God is able to put some good into this year and into the world for the enjoyment of God's children, who have been bought with the price of the precious blood of God's Son. When God created the world, God looked at it and said it was good. Good things are built into life and creation. All we need is enough faith, vision, and get-up-and-go to find them.

When we serve a God whose pleasure it is to give us the kingdom, why are we afraid to have great expectations in life? Our foreparents didn't feel this way. They used to sing:

Believe I'll run on, and see what the end will be;
'Cause something's at the end just waiting for me.

If with all they faced, if with the restrictions that were imposed upon them, they could still believe that life held something good, even if those things were farther down the road, why can't we in our time, with fewer obstacles and more opportunities, believe that life holds some good things for us? Why can't we have some great expectations? Oh, where is our faith?

I know that some of us may sincerely believe that life has passed us by. If we had married a different person or had not married as early as we did or had stayed in school; if we had chosen a different profession or started our career a little earlier or grabbed a certain business opportunity; if we had accepted the promotion that was offered to us or had been willing to move to a certain location, things would be so different for us now. If we had not wasted some of our younger years and opportunities; if we had taken care of our bodies a little earlier or listened to what our parents, grandparents, teachers, and preachers, and some of the older folk were trying to tell us; if we could go back and start over again, life would be so different. If we had been born to different parents and raised in different circumstances; if we had been given someone else's talents or breaks, then there is no telling how far we could have gone. But the die has been cast for us, and there is nothing that anyone can do about it. No one can turn the clock back, and no one can exchange our place for another. But right where we are, no matter how old or young we are, no matter how much water has flowed under the bridge, we can still have some great expectations. The process and the word of God can still be fulfilled in our lives. This moment of time and the year in which we stand can still hold some glad surprises and good things for us.

　　This is what makes the story of Anna in the text so precious. According to the Scriptures, Anna was a prophetess. In the Hebrew Bible, Miriam, Deborah, Huldah, and Isaiah's wife were known as prophetesses. While there are several references to the women in the early Christian community who prophesied, Anna is the only woman in the New Testament given the title of prophetess, except for the wicked Jezebel, who, according to the book of Revelation, called herself a prophetess (Revelation 2:20).[1] "To prophesy simply means to proclaim a divine message . . . and Anna was one through whom God spoke to others."[2] She had lost her husband while yet a young woman and never remarried. Estimates of her age range from eighty-four to one hundred and three, and according to the Scriptures, "She did not depart from the temple, worshiping with fasting and praying night and day" (Luke 2:37).

　　Some undoubtedly looked at Anna and assumed that she was living a dull life and had nothing to look forward to but death. Two of the greatest mistakes we can ever make are the assumptions that a life of holiness is dull and that church people and old people have nothing to look forward to but death. Holiness is about living; sin is about dying.

1Raymond Brown, *The Birth of the Messiah: A Commentary on the Infancy Narratives in Matthew and Luke* (New York: Doubleday, 1979), p. 441.

2Herbert Lockyer, *All the Women of the Bible* (Grand Rapids: Zondervan, 1967), p. 30.

Anyone who joins the church because he or she is solely making preparations to die is off base. We join the church because we're preparing to live, because we have some great expectations about what we can become and do through Christ who strengthens us. If we are living in the center of God's will with hopes and dreams, we can't be idle and won't have a lot of time to spend on a morbid preoccupation with death. The old spiritual says:

I keep so busy serving my Jesus . . .
I keep so busy working for the kingdom . . .
I ain't got time to die.[3]

Anna, as a very old woman, lived an exciting life of holiness; she lived a life of fasting and prayer. When we fast and pray, we can have great expectations. People who have no great expectations can't have much of a prayer life because prayer breeds hope. Praying is not an act of desperation, but of hope. When we pray, we're not in despair because we can't handle the situation, we're in hope because we're coming to Somebody who is able to do what we can't.

Anna had hope and a dream that kept her going. We live by our dreams and hopes. When the present is in turmoil, all that keeps us going are our dreams and hopes. Show me a person without dreams and hopes, and I'll show you a person, no matter how young or how old, who may be physically alive but inwardly dead. Anna, like all the faithful believers in Israel at that time, longed and waited, prayed and fasted for the coming of God's anointed. Thus, year after year, she stayed in the temple with the hope that soon and very soon the Deliverer would come. She didn't know if she would see him or when he would come, but she had great expectations.

Finally, one day while in the temple, she saw a young couple standing before Simeon, who was holding their little baby in his arms. Simeon, like Anna, was an old saint with a great expectation. His one desire was to see the Messiah before he died, and God's Spirit had revealed to him that his request would be granted. When Anna saw Simeon praising God for the Babe he held in his arms, she knew that his

---

3From "Ain't Got Time to Die," traditional spiritual.

prayer had been answered. Anna also gave thanks to God and then testified to others who had great expectations and who also looked for the redemption of Israel.

When Simeon saw the baby Jesus, he said, "Lord, now lettest thou thy servant depart in peace, according to thy word; for mine eyes have seen thy salvation . . ." (Luke 2:29). Anna, however, prayed no such prayer, but went forth to tell others that the Promised One had come. Life does not have to end because our great expectations have come to pass, for we can then have a great testimony. As our expectations and dreams kept us going, our testimonies can strengthen others. Our story changes from what we hoped to what we know, from what we've been promised to what we have received, from what we believed by faith to what we've experienced for ourselves. Great expectations lead to great testimonies, and when we have great testimonies, life is still exciting.

Anna had been in the temple for many years, and one day her faith was rewarded. I doubt that the sun shone any longer or brighter or hotter that day. I doubt that the wind blew any differently or the birds sang any differently. I doubt that she saw any signs in the heavens that indicated to her that something special was going to happen to her that day. From all outward appearances the day that she saw Jesus was probably like any other day. Yet that day was unlike any other she had experienced. This very day may be the most important day in our lives. From all outward appearances it may look and feel like any other day. This year may have started out like any other year, but this year can be a very special one for us. We never know when the Lord will reward our faith. At a time and place when we least expect, the Lord may have a special blessing, a special message, a special vision or revelation for us. That's why we must always live with great expectations of God's Spirit at work in our lives, great expectations of miracles, great expectations of answered prayer, and great expectations of salvation.

To be truly Christian is to live with great expectations, for Jesus told us that he was going away and that he was coming back and bringing the rewards for faithfulness with him. We know not the day nor the hour when he will come; therefore, we are to watch for our redemption to draw nigh. I don't mind telling you that I have some great expectations because "the Lord has promised good to me, his word my hope secures."[4] Therefore, I'm claiming this year by faith. Do you have any great expectations this year? Are you still singing this as your theme song:

What peaceful hours I then enjoyed!
How sweet their memory still!
But they have left an aching void
The world can never fill.[5]

Maybe we ought to start singing:

Something good is going to happen to [me],
Happen to [me] this very day;
Something good is going to happen to [me]—
Jesus of Nazareth is passing [my] way.[6]

---

[4]From "Amazing Grace," by John Newton.

[5]From "O for a Closer Walk with God," by William Cowper.

[6]From "Something Good Is Going to Happen to You," by Ralph Carmichael. Copyright © 1969 by BudJohn Songs (ASCAP). Administered by CMI. International copyright secured. All rights reserved. Used by permission.

3

The Samaritan Woman:
Love Without Limits

John 4:1–30
Suzan D. Johnson Cook

And at this point His disciples came, and they marveled that He talked with a woman; yet no one said, "What do You seek?" or, "Why are You talking with her?" The woman then left her waterpot, went her way into the city, and said to the men, "Come, see a man who told me all things I ever did. Could this be the Christ?" (John 4:27 – 29, NKJV).

It is interesting how life finds us in the most unusual circumstances just in the midst of doing that which is ordinary. Just last week I went to Washington, D.C., to fulfill a commitment I had made more than a year ago to preach to a convention. Although I pride myself on trying to find out as much as possible about an audience prior to meeting them, I can honestly say that I did not know the full depth of this particular one. It turned out that most of those attending the convention were Southern Baptist pastors and laity who had a vision for church growth and renewal. Once I realized the setting I was in, I was dazzled by the fact that years ago, the Southern Baptists had split with the American Baptists over the issue of slavery, and more recently they had taken a very firm stand against women in the ordained ministry. Yet here I was, performing a regular function as a preacher and standing tall as an African American woman, a descendant of slavery, and an ordained minister of the gospel. Time with God does indeed bring about change. At the conclusion of the service, several women, both lay and clergy, tightly grasped my hand, expressing thanks for a spiritual

15

breakthrough. They had not been prepared to receive me well; in fact, they expressed that they had come with their limitations to be placed on themselves and me, but that God used me to minister to them.

As I flew back home, I was reading this text and trying to envision how the woman at the well may have felt when she needed a breakthrough in her own life. Here she was, doing an ordinary chore—drawing water from a well, an essential element for functioning within any society. Women who were more "well off" usually had someone to get water for them, and even women in the lower economic status usually did not wait until the middle of the day when the sun was at its peak to do this chore. Perhaps this woman chose to come to the well at this "off hour" because she had been outcast by most of her peers, for it was obvious to them that she lived against the standards and norms of their religious community. She lived with a man. And to further complicate this scenario, she was a Samaritan woman, a mixture of five different nations—a race ignored and almost repulsed by the Jews. She had been denied even her basic human rights and dignity. By all standards and logic, nothing extraordinary was supposed to happen to or for her on that day. She was just drawing water from this well that stood on the site where Jacob had been, and where tradition had been standing for a long while.

And as Jesus came by, we see the traditional so inextricably juxtaposed with the untraditional. On this day this Samaritan woman was about to draw her water, about one o'clock in the afternoon, about midday, when the sun was high and sweat was pouring down her brow. This same day Jesus had a trip to make. He had a choice of two different directions or routes to follow. The One who directs all steps and our paths, the Guiding Light, found himself with a choice to make. He could follow the same route that all the Jews before and after him would follow, which would mean bypassing Samaria altogether, or he could take a more direct route in which he would have to confront Samaria and all of its intricacies, complexities, and all that it represented. Jesus on this day sought to go through Samaria. Just as the woman, he was also hot, and sweat was beginning to bead upon his brow. He needed a drink of water, and as divine providence would have it, the only one at the well was this woman of Samaria, whom others had intentionally ignored.

As Jesus approached the well, the woman probably assumed that he, being both a Jew and a man, would not confer with her, a woman of Samaria. First of all, it was against the religious tradition for a man to speak publicly with a woman; and it also violated the cultural norm because these two ethnic groups did not intermingle. Yet Jesus spoke to her. Racism and sexism were set aside in the presence of one who said, "Whosoever will, let her come." Astonished, amazed, grateful, and perhaps even paralyzed with fear, this Samaritan woman at the well responded, and a dialogue began that would change her life forever. Jesus had her confront her sins and do a self-assessment, not for his benefit, but for her own. No one obviously had ever had her look closely at herself, for no one bothered to see if the situation in which she found herself had been comfortable for her or not. No questions were ever asked of her; no compassion had ever been shown her; and therefore, no response had ever been given. But on this particular day, with this particular man, things were different. Jesus confronted her and demonstrated that with acknowledgment, confession, and belief, salvation and transformation could come. She had to face the facts, as painful or as deniable as they might be. But with her willingness, the seeds were planted for the beginning of a powerful witness. The ensuing dialogue allowed some issues to surface that neither she nor anyone else had ever been brave enough to deal with. She had been living in sin, and unless she was willing to both confront and change her way of living, she could not go forward and have what Jesus had for her, nor do what was intended for her to do. Nor would she be able to worship God so that power would be able to come to her life, because only true worshipers are able to experience God's fullness.

One of the first points of true worship is self-confrontation—being ready for God's cleansing and healing, coupled with the release of that which has burdened one down. And God is a God of "no excuse." God will not allow us to transfer onto others that which belongs to us and which we need to deal with ourselves. The issue was not so much about husbands and wives or living arrangements as it was about her soul salvation, that is, being in a right relationship with God and with the others with whom she would be involved so that her life would be set free. For the first time, her liberation came. As I read this text, I began to think of the beginning of Jesus' ministry, when he went to the temple, turned to the Isaiah passage, and began to read, "the Spirit of the Lord is upon me . . . to set at liberty those who are oppressed. . . ." A Samaritan woman was released of some pressure that had become so bottled up inside her that she could not live the abundant life. Jesus came so that we could have life and have it more abundantly. We recognize that truth from a request for a drink of water from One who was and is the Living Water. New life came for one who had needed it for a long time.

Yet this is where I believe the real power of the story begins. Even though Jesus broke through the barriers and myths of racism and sexism that had previously existed, this woman and Jesus still had to be confronted by others who had not been present at the time of conversion.

In this life, many who come to worship leave feeling full of joy and empowered to battle the many forces that plague their lives. Yet often, even before they leave the sacred walls of the sanctuary, they find resistance to who they are or what they represent. This means, then, that the test of true conversion does not only lie in the encountering of Jesus nor solely with the worship experience, for these are both personal experiences. The true tests follow when we are forced to interact with and engage others, some of whom may have been with Jesus, others who may have not.

Almost immediately after her conversion, this Samaritan woman and Jesus had to face the disciples, who had not been present. The disciples were astonished that he was going against tradition—that is, he was speaking to a person of a different gender who was also outside of his race. They saw firsthand that Jesus had chosen to challenge a tradition in order to do God's will. This raises the question, Does one who is in God bow or break because of societal and peer pressure, or does one continue to do what he or she believes to be right in the eyes of God?

This is the same issue Jesus had to deal with in Matthew 22, when a young lawyer asked him what were the greatest commandments. Jesus answered that right relationships with God and with your neighbor were the greatest, for on these two hung all the law and the prophets.

I marvel at the way the response comes in this text in John, for it now comes from an empowered woman of Jesus who had a testimony and a witness. She had come with a horrible past, but could leave with a bright future. Her response was, "Come see a man who told me all that I ever did."

In other words, the focus had been all wrong. It is not whether a certain race or gender is able to do certain things or be involved in certain events. The issue is, Are those who have encountered Jesus willing to take stands that represent him, despite the powers and pressures that remain present within societal norms and traditions? She had come with a waterpot and left with a witness; she was now able to give God the glory because she had told Jesus her story. She could now adore him because she no longer ignored herself.

Floods of memories began to surface as I delved into the depths of this passage. I remembered the countless times many of my brothers who represent a conference of Baptists in New York City, which supposedly represents justice for all, could not see past their own sexism. They will, for example, call myself and other sisters in ministry to join them in their marches, battles, and cries for justice at City Hall, against apartheid, homelessness, and other dilemmas, yet still to this day do not permit women clergy to join their conference. Therefore, I, as a senior pastor who trains students, both female and male, in seminary, can attend and see my male students be received with joy into the conference; yet I, who trained them, am considered insignificant and must remain silent.

Yet, as the disciples in this biblical story, my male colleagues were not present when I encountered Jesus; and like the Samaritan woman, I must still use my witness and testimony, despite the tradition, perhaps not at a well, but in places where living water is able to flow.

I am also reminded of the many times when male colleagues in seminary turned their backs on me and my sisters because of peer pressure from other men who chastised them for being involved with a "woman preacher." Again, barriers of sexism need to be discarded.

Sexism and racism are often partners that oppose African American women in employment searches, interviews, school functions, and professional affairs. Still, I have a witness that must be spread abroad about a person named Jesus, who chose to come in my direction—One who symbolically continues to make requests of me for drinks of water from the wells from which I draw and receive my strength.

I have been empowered by the choice Jesus made to come into my life. Therefore, I constantly find myself trying to make the choices I feel would be pleasing to him as I function in this place where I find myself.

The Samaritans still exist; only the names and boundaries have changed. Criticisms are always prevalent. But I cannot only raise the question, "Can this be the Christ?"; I can firmly and confidently answer in the affirmative: Yes, this is the Christ, who makes me confront who I am, not dwell on the sins and mistakes I have committed. He empowers and renews me to go forward with a story of One who does indeed transform and bless our lives.

4

The Samaritan Woman:
She Left Her Water Pitcher

John 4:27–30
William D. Watley

It was a hot summer's day when the Samaritan woman came with her pitcher to draw water from Jacob's well as she had done so often. As she approached the well, there was one thing on her mind, and that was to fill her pitcher with the cool water of Jacob's well and get out of the blistering noonday sun as quickly as possible. She paid little attention to the stranger who was sitting there alone resting himself. His disciples, his friends, had gone into a nearby town to buy food. Thus, he sat alone at the well at the noon hour. If this woman had come in the evening, in the cool of the day, which was the usual time for gathering water, there would have been so many others milling about that she might not have noticed Jesus. However, because they were alone, Jesus was able to speak more openly with her and she with him. We should never fear being alone with the Lord. There are some things that can only be revealed to us when we are alone with God.

This woman who had come to the well to discharge a daily personal task of drawing water did not realize the privilege, opportunity, or blessing that would soon be hers. Here, sitting alone, was the Promised One of God, who was not only the hope of Israel but also of all humanity. Here, sitting alone, was the one who carried within his heart the mission and bore upon his shoulders the task of humankind's redemption. Jesus sat there quietly, patiently, almost

as if he were waiting just for her. And I believe he was waiting for her. There are no accidental meetings with God.
Things just don't happen without forethought with God.
Heaven moves with intentionality and purpose. We are
where we are for a purpose, and sometimes it is only as we
spend time alone with the Lord that we discover what that
purpose is. As the woman prepared to draw water, the
stranger spoke to her and asked for a drink. She looked at
him somewhat startled because a closer examination of his
features and his accent revealed that he was not a Samaritan but a Galilean Jew. As the Scriptures inform us, "the
Jews have no dealings with the Samaritans."

There was a long and interesting history of the ten-
sion between these two peoples. The land of Palestine,
though only about 120 miles long from north to south, had
within its borders three distinct divisions of its territory. In
the extreme north was the area known as Galilee; in the
extreme south was the area known as Judea; and in the
center dividing them was the region known as Samaria.
In 722 B.C., the Assyrians had invaded the kingdom of Samaria, had transported the bulk of the population to Media,
and had brought other subject peoples into Samaritan territory and settled them there. The Jews who were removed
from Samaria never returned, but were absorbed in the nations to which they had been taken and became the ten lost
tribes of Israel. The original Samaritans who had been left
in Palestine began intermarrying with those who had been
imported into their land. Thus the Samaritans lost the racial purity that was so important to the theological perspective of the ancient orthodox Jew.

In 587 B.C., those Jews of the south, in Judea, were invaded by the Babylonians and transported to Babylon. But
unlike their northern kinspeople, they were never assimi-
lated into the culture of their captors. As Psalm 137 tells us,
they hung their harps upon the willow trees and wept when
they remembered Zion. They continued to preserve their
culture, affirm their faith, and remain a community apart,
even in Babylon. When Babylon fell, many of them returned
to Palestine and to Judea to reclaim the land of their heritage. The Judean Jews never forgave their northern kin of
Samaria for intermixing with persons of other races and
cultures and considered them not to be Jews at all. The
Jews of Samaria, relying upon their own history and tradition, believed themselves to be as Jewish as those who

dwelt in Judea. For centuries the Judeans and Samaritans coexisted side by side, within the same land, in a relationship that was strained at best and openly hostile at worst.

The geography of Palestine made it impossible for them to avoid each other. Since Samaria lay between Judea and Galilee, the quickest and most direct way from one to the other was through Samaria, about a three-day journey. To avoid Samaria, the alternate route was to cross the Jordan River, follow the eastern bank, and then recross the Jordan at a point north of Samaria, and enter into Galilee. This route would take twice as long. An orthodox Jew would take the farther route to keep his feet from touching Samaritan soil, but Jesus took the direct route.

If there is any one thing that the New Testament is clear about, it is that Jesus is direct. As truth, he is direct and straight. Truth does not ponder and pet, waver and wander; truth is direct. Jesus is direct in dealing with us. We do not have to go through a host of intermediaries to get to him; he hears and answers us directly and personally. He is direct and straight in his work. He is not sidetracked into longstanding controversies, and he doesn't waste time on pettiness. Jesus understands that life is too short for game playing, hesitation, and procrastination. When one considers all that he accomplished within just three short years of ministry, one witnesses the life of a Savior who was direct in engaging the task of redemption, who swerved neither to the right nor the left.

When the woman at the well responded to Jesus' request, she answered the only way she knew—with the defensiveness and prejudice that had been instilled in her from childhood. She said, "How is it that you, a Jew, ask a drink of me, a woman of Samaria?" (John 4:9). "Have you no regard for social standards or historic attitudes? Where is your sense of propriety? Don't you realize that because our people do not get along, we are not supposed to like each other, talk to each other, love each other, or relate to each other in any way?" (author's paraphrase).

I believe that God is very patient with people such as this because God realizes that many of us don't know of other ways to act. We have been hurt or rejected and don't know any other way to be than mean, vengeful, defensive, supersensitive, and distrustful. Blacks and whites have been at odds for so long that we don't know how to approach one another initially without suspicion or hostility. We even view as strange those who try to bridge the gap or who refuse to let historic differences between groups determine the character of their personal relationships.

Although he was a product of his times, as we all are, Jesus was not a victim of his times. He never let custom determine his behavior or society set his standards or tradition or history color his attitudes. He accepted people and situations as they were and then pointed them in new directions. Jesus did not even address the issue of historic hostility between Samaritan and Jew, but began immediately to pursue the issue that was uppermost in his mind. He was not interested in longstanding feuds, but in reconciliation. He was not primarily interested in either Samaria or Judea, but in the kingdom of God. Or, to quote one preacher, "when Jesus comes to a situation, he doesn't take sides, he takes over." He directed the conversation toward higher things and, in essence, told the woman, "If you knew the gift of God, and who it is that asks for a drink, then you also would have forgotten about custom and propriety and asked him for a drink and he would have given you living water." The woman said, "Sir, you have nothing to draw with, and the well is deep; where do you get that living water? Are you greater than our father Jacob, who gave us the well, and drank from it himself, and his sons, and his cattle?" (vv. 11 – 12).

Jesus said, "You still don't understand the nature of the water I am talking about, but I'll give you a sample of it. I'll give you some drops of truth. Go, call your husband" (author's paraphrase of vv. 13 – 16). The woman answered, "I have no husband" (v. 17). Jesus said to her directly, poignantly, truthfully, "You are right in saying, 'I have no husband'; for you have had five husbands, and he whom you now have is not your husband; this you said truly" (v. 16). The woman said, as she set her water pitcher down, "Sir, I perceive that you are a prophet" (v. 19). Here was a woman with a questionable past, who came obviously living in sin, but who recognized the fact that she was in the presence of God's messenger. When we truly represent what we say we believe, sinners and saints alike will know we belong to God.

The woman said, "Our fathers worshiped on this mountain; and you say that in Jerusalem is the place where men ought to worship" (v. 20). Jesus said, "I'm going to give you another drop of this living water that is the vibrant and living worship of God, who is truth. True worship of the true God is not tied to any one place or building or group or church. For the hour is coming when neither on this mountain will you worship the Father" (author's paraphrase of vv.21 – 22). "The hour is coming, and now is, when the true worshipers will worship the Father in spirit and truth, for such the Father seeks to worship him. God is spirit, and those who worship him must worship him in spirit and in truth" (vv.23 – 24). The woman said to him, "I know that Messiah is coming (he who is called Christ); and when he comes, he will show us all things" (v.25). Jesus said, "I'm going to give you another drop of the living water. I'm going to introduce you to the One who can give you the peace you've been seeking; One who can give you the contentment, happiness, and security that none of those five husbands could give. I'm going to give you knowledge of One who alone can save, sanctify, heal, and redeem you. It is I who speaks to you" (author's paraphrase of v.26).

At that point the disciples returned from their errands, and although they were surprised to see Jesus publicly conversing with a Samaritan woman, they said nothing. The glow on the woman's face must have told them that something glorious was happening in her life. I imagine that her face was bright with the joy that comes when we discover something that we've been searching for for a long time. She had discovered truth; she had discovered true worship; she had discovered Jesus. And so she left her water pitcher to tell others what she had found. She left what she brought in her hands and took away what she had received in her heart. She didn't get what she had come for—she came for physical water from Jacob's well to quench a temporary thirst. She left with living water from Jesus which satisfies the eternal longing of the soul.

When she came to the well, all she could think about was filling her pitcher; when she left, all she could think about was Jesus. Her experience with Jesus overshadowed that which she brought, and it gave to her a new perception of herself, a new understanding of God, and a new reason for living. With uncontrollable joy she went to spread the news about Jesus.

She, of all people, spread the news about Jesus. She whose five marriages had scandalized the community; of all people, she who was involved in an illicit affair; of all people, she who had been the victim of so much talk and the brunt of so many jokes; of all people, she who had been shunned by some of the more respectable women of the community; of all people—she spread the news about Jesus. See her as she ran through the streets of the community proclaiming, "I've found him, I've found understanding for my failures, forgiveness for my transgressions, purpose for my meager talents, usefulness and meaning for my wasted and unprofitable life. I've found a Savior who cares" (author's words). "Come, see a man who told me all that I ever did. Can this be the Christ?" (v.29).

As we take note of our lives, we must admit that too many of us are carrying pitchers of ill will, pitchers of guilt, pitchers of reservation and suspicion. We've been carrying these pitchers a long time. If in the course of time anything ever disappears out of those pitchers, we go back to earthly pools and fill them again. A pitcher holds everything. A sieve allows some things to pass through; a filter processes what passes through; but a pitcher holds everything as it is. Some of us remember every unkind word or deed or hurt we've ever received. Some of us are just waiting for the right moment to get even. But he who gives and is the living water is speaking to us in the words of the gospel and telling us that it is time we leave pitchers of vengeance and ill will behind. Some of us made a mistake, and everyone has forgiven us except us. We walk around weighted down with our own guilt and sense of failure. So we made a mistake. So what? We can't undo the past, but we can do something about the present. It's time we leave our pitchers of guilt and self-pity behind. Some of us could do more and give more of ourselves; but since we have been hurt and deceived before, we're holding back lest we be disappointed again. God can't get the full glory out of our lives when we hold back. We've been nursing our hurt feelings long enough. It's time we leave pitchers of reservation and suspicion behind.

I know it's not easy to leave pitchers behind, especially ones we've been carrying so long. There is someone, however, who can help us lay them aside. The Samaritan woman did not plan to leave her pitcher; she just became so wrapped up in Jesus that the pitcher paled in its importance. She understood that there was something more vital for her to be doing with her life at that moment than simply filling her pitcher. She was in such a hurry to spread the news about Jesus that carrying it would have been a hindrance, so she left it at Jesus' feet and ran into the city.

The key to leaving pitchers is found in a new and dynamic relationship with Jesus, who turns us inside out, upside down, and makes us brand new. You don't have to be burdened with old water pitchers. Leave them at Jesus' feet. When we meet Jesus, things that once upset us don't upset us anymore. People that once got next to us don't bother us anymore. Words and deeds that once hurt us and discouraged us and made us cry don't cut as deeply as before. Why? Because Jesus gives us a new way of walking, a new way of talking, and a new reason for living. He gives us a new heart, a new song, new joy, new hope, new courage, new patience, new understanding, new forgiveness, new strength, new courage, a new being, new vision, and new life. With Jesus' help the Samaritan woman left her water pitcher. With Jesus' help we too can leave ours.

5

The Woman with the Issue of Blood:
Somebody Touched Me

Luke 8:40–48
Suzan D. Johnson Cook

Now when Jesus returned, the crowd welcomed him, for they were all waiting for him. And there came a man named Jairus, who was a ruler of the synagogue; and falling at Jesus' feet he besought him to come to his house, for he had an only daughter, about twelve years of age, and she was dying.

As he went, the people pressed round him. And a woman who had had a flow of blood for twelve years and could not be healed by any one, came up behind him, and touched the fringe of his garment; and immediately her flow of blood ceased. And Jesus said, "Who was it that touched me?" When all denied it, Peter said, "Master, the multitudes surround you and press upon you!" But Jesus said, "Someone touched me; for I perceive that power has gone forth from me." And when the woman saw that she was not hidden, she came trembling, and falling down before him declared in the presence of all the people why she had touched him, and how she had been immediately healed. And he said to her, "Daughter, your faith has made you well; go in peace" (Luke 8:40–48).

We live in a world that is filled with many opportunities for rejection and hardships. That is why many persons spend so much time and money trying to be accepted by what they perceive to be the societal norms, because rejection is difficult to accept. That, perhaps, is why there are so many auxiliaries within the body of the organized church—to provide opportunities for many who would otherwise feel all

29

alone to find some acceptance of themselves by others within a safe and close environment.

Parents often try to have their children involved in many activities—piano lessons, drama or dance lessons, sports teams, Girl Scouts or Boy Scouts—as a means of having them learn how to "fit in." The older the children become, the more they can make their own decisions and choices, but the pattern has already been set. In high school and college, students try out memberships on various boards and committees, trying to be included in what they think are the important activities. These range from fraternities and sororities to yearbook committees and various other social and civic events. There seems to be nothing worse or more humiliating than to be excluded from certain events, for exclusion signifies that the majority group does not consider a person good enough or popular enough to be included.

Many adults may still feel excluded, and sometimes this is true even within the body of Christ. I have spent countless Saturdays and evenings at workshops and retreats with Christians who shared their pain of not feeling wanted.

If you have ever experienced any feelings of rejection as a child or as an adult; if you can recall a time when you did not feel particularly welcome as a part of a group, then perhaps you can identify with the central character of today's story. She is referred to as the woman with the issue of blood. She had been so stigmatized that no one bothered to find out her name or what she preferred to be called. Everyone identified her according to her illness and not according to her contributions or her self-worth.

She was a woman who lived at a time when the Levitical laws were in existence. During this time it was important for a woman not only to be identified by family connections but also to function within the context that had been created for the women of this society. Most women did their chores and activities along with a group of other women. But this woman had no connection to her family or her peers. In fact, these Levitical laws by which she had to live considered her an unclean woman, which meant that wherever she went, no one else was, by law, able to associate with her. She had to do everything independently and alone.

Imagine, if you will, not being able to drink out of the

public drinking fountains or hold conversations with neighborhood friends and associates. Imagine not being able to dine at the public eateries or even to use the utensils that everyone else used. Her situation was even more pronounced and demeaning than that which was described for people with leprosy. At least they lived in communes and had contact with others like themselves. But this woman had no one. She was alone and lonely. And she had been bleeding (hemorrhaging) for twelve long years. Nothing and no one could stop it. In fact, according to the Gospel of Mark, it troubled her so much that she had spent all her life's earnings and savings on physicians, trying to find a cure, but to no avail. She needed someone who would understand how she was feeling. She was neither invited, welcomed, nor included.

Well, on a particular day, she found out, through her own limited network and sources and by the prevailing discussions she overheard, that Jesus was coming to the immediate vicinity. She had heard the stories about his healing and deliverance, about his bringing relief to those who were in need, and in her desperation, which was coupled with her hope, she perceived that if she could get close enough to where he was, then maybe she stood a chance for the first time of being helped. Desperately she made her way to the shores of the Sea of Gennesaret. This was a familiar and common place where Jesus often took his disciples for retreat.

As Jesus' boat approached the shores, a large crowd, perhaps in the thousands, gathered. (As I read this story, I began wondering if it was a crowd larger than that which gathered for the historic coming of Nelson Mandela to my region.) Heroes and heroines often attract large crowds when news of their arrival spreads. And this crowd no doubt included some of the same people who had previously rejected this lonely woman—persons who may have said some unkind words; persons who may have refused to sit where she sat; neighbors who made it clear by their body language that they would not interact with her; persons who would not and did not challenge the very laws that were created to ostracize her. They may have even, at this very moment, with Jesus so close by, still tried to block her from being healed and from receiving a blessing. Yet she persevered. And pushing through the crowd, she found a place to stand, hoping that Jesus would pass her way.

But just as this woman found a place to stand, Jairus, a ruler of the synagogue, fell at Jesus' feet and begged him to come to his house to heal his twelve-year-old daughter, who lay dying. A father was in distress, and a bleeding woman in desperation. Hopeless and helpless, partners in tribulation. What do you suppose was going through the woman's head, hearing that perhaps Jesus would have to make a choice about which way to go? Maybe he would change his direction or delay his interaction with this crowd, and maybe she would not be able to get near him.

But because God is a God of life for all—those who lay dying and also those who have been living with imposed death; those who are helpless; and those for whom hope is uttered—Jesus demonstrated that both situations could be dealt with. On the way to Jairus's house, Jesus came to where the needs were. The woman managed to touch the hem of his garment, and in doing so, her healing came. Because she was able to connect with Jesus' power, for the first time in twelve long years her identity crisis was over—her victory had come. She was able to be made whole.

Think of the countless nights that the woman had probably cried herself to sleep or looked upon herself with self-hatred or self-pity. Now she had been made whole. But wholeness comes with knowing who the healer is. She had to acknowledge Jesus as the one who had been responsible for her wholeness. Jesus, the one who would become the wounded healer, was used to heal the wounded.

As I read and reread the woman's story, I certainly could not but help placing myself in her story, trying to remember the circumstances in which I felt left out in my own life. I recalled the times in a private, exclusive prep school when I was one of only two black students in an entire grade, when because of my skin color and the other students' lack of cultural sensitivity, I was often rejected, despite the numerous organizations in which I participated. I began to think of the many ways I dealt with the stress and the stress-related illnesses that would begin to creep up into the lives of minority students and how often we would not have channels by which to vent our stress because there were some unwritten laws that prevented others from associating with us. In dealing with my own pain, which had probably been buried for as long as this biblical woman had been bleeding, I was able to identify ways in which the organized church and I, as a minister of the gospel, must be sensitive to the needs of others within our midst to whom we minister. Churches of Christ must be places of wholeness so that their people will be able to touch Jesus in the center of our crowds, otherwise known as the community of believers of the faith. This is particularly true with our modern-day issues of blood, more commonly known as AIDS. How many victims of this fatal and tragic disease have tried to break through the crowds? The written and the unwritten laws that society has placed on them subtly suggest that they are "unclean."

As I came into my own wholeness, God made me aware of this illness in a personal way just two years ago. I was on my way to a Bible study class that I conducted at Mariners' Temple Baptist Church when I received a telephone call from a musician whom I had known in the past. He had played an instrument at a church where I ministered, and through that encounter we had become relatively close. He said that he was in the hospital for a routine checkup, but he asked if I would bring and serve him Communion. Certainly this was not a bizarre request to make of a minister of the gospel, but it was not the type of request he had ever made of me before. And so I consented to go. As I arrived at the ward where he was, I began to see the familiar sign that many hospitals post to indicate that there is an infectious disease with which we should exercise serious caution. As I approached his bed and saw a man who did not appear to be the same man I once knew, I awkwardly tried to minister to him. Just then a nurse came in to take his temperature, which allowed me a chance to excuse myself. I found the nurses' station and inquired whether or not my friend's malady was the disease I suspected it was. A nurse confirmed that it was AIDS and instructed me on the necessary precautions to take. Well, I was so dumbfounded, because of the stories I had heard about the disease, that although I returned and sat by his bedside and listened to his stories about rejection from friends and family and about dying, I never did serve him Communion because I was paralyzed with fear.

When I left the hospital, I wrestled with the idea that I had not fulfilled his request. I tried to call hospital chaplains and others to take him Communion for me, but for whatever reason, I was not making the necessary connections. I was able to share my own uneasiness with my Bible class that evening, and they were able to be a crowd that ministered to me and propelled me to go back and try again. I did go back, and I was able to serve him Communion. He wept and said that for the first time in a long time, he felt whole. I imagine that was how the woman with a blood issue felt— that someone for the first time in a long time was able not only to hear and feel her pain but also to participate in her new joy. My Bible class was indeed the Christ presence I needed on that evening.

My friend died the next day. Despite my grief, I was thankful that God had given me another chance to deal with this modern-day issue of blood, reminding me of my own inadequacies, but also reminding me of how it felt when I was rejected in my own life and how sensitive I must be not to consciously reject others. The experience also reminded me of one more important lesson—that neither my whole- ness nor your wholeness is dependent on the approval of crowds of others whom we deem to be the dominant voices in society. But best of all, our wholeness comes from a divine / human combination—our working in connection with God, who can penetrate even the thickest crowd and see about our own needs. For it is in our healing that we be- come the agents for change and wholeness for the very crowds that may have rejected us. What happens at the end of this story is also critical for this text. The woman with the blood issue no longer had gloom to report. Instead she had a testimony of healed life, a testimony about one who can stop a burdensome situation and replace it with a testimony of good news.

Because of maturity and spiritual breakthrough, I have now forgiven those from that prep school and learned how to help them be more sensitive for this new generation that will enter their school. Already I have been invited to be a speaker at a career day and have been asked to work with recruitment and with the alumni association. In my own way, with Christ's help, healing has come for both them and myself.

Because of the close encounter with my friend who died of AIDS, I was able to minister effectively to a family in my congregation who lost a loved one to the same disease. And God was able to use my eulogy of this person as a way to help my congregation and community deal with this modern-day issue of blood.

From a woman who was identified only by an illness, a woman with an issue of blood, she became a whole creature, named and identified with Jesus—from doomed to delivered disciple. What a wonderful change in her life had been wrought.

Thanks be to God for God's speakable and unspeakable gifts.

6

The Woman with the Issue of Blood: *Who Touched Me?*

Mark 5:21–34
William D. Watley

Today's subject is the response of Jesus to someone who had rubbed him the right way. "Who touched me?"—this question seemed strange to a number of those who heard it because when he asked it, Jesus was in the midst of a crowd. He was on his way to the home of Jairus, a local synagogue administrator, to minister to the daughter of this distressed father. A crowd was following Jesus, and crowds by their very nature, intrude upon our space, bumping into us and rubbing shoulders with us. That's why it's important, as I've often said before, that we are careful about the crowd with which we travel.

Never believe that we can travel with the wrong crowd and not be touched by it. Someone was eminently correct in saying, "Bad company ruins good manners." Even the strongest saint can be adversely affected by the wrong crowd. It's hard to consistently hang around with a crowd of drinkers, cursers, smokers, drug addicts, gossipers, pessimists, and unbelievers and not be influenced by the standards of those crowds.

Many a parent has said to me, "My child isn't bad; he just fell in with the wrong crowd." If Rehoboam, the son of Solomon and his successor to the throne, had not listened to the wrong crowd, he would not have made the wrong administrative decision that resulted in the split of the kingdom of Israel into the northern part known as Israel and the southern part known as Judah. If the prodigal son had associated with a different crowd, he might not have ended up in a hog pen. When our Lord was being tried, Peter did what he considered to be the unbelievable. He denied knowing Jesus because he was hanging out with the wrong crowd.

The crowd we travel with can make a difference in our lives. One of the principles of Alcoholics, Narcotics, Sexaholics, Smokers, Overeaters, and Gamblers Anonymous is that the crowd we associate with can make a difference in our lives. If the crowd we associate with is supportive of our efforts to do the right thing, then that support can be our salvation. That's what the fellowship of the church is at its best—a support crowd for those who are trying to do the right thing. We're not a perfect crowd; neither are we called to be a judgmental and condemning crowd of those who have made mistakes or who have weaknesses. We're not called to be a negative or fault-finding crowd, or a self-righteous or mean-spirited crowd, or an arrogant or an elitist crowd—but a support crowd for those who are trying to do the right thing.

If the crowd we associate with is supportive of our wrongdoing, then that crowd can be detrimental to our souls. Sometimes we hold to certain crowds because we consider them to be our friends. I'm not telling anyone to get rid of their friends if they are really friends, but sometimes we need to take a long hard look at those we consider to be our friends. What are our so-called friends about, and what are our so-called friendships about? One night when my son, Matthew, and I were driving down the street, we saw two teen-age boys walking together. Matthew said to me, "I know them; they go to my school, and both of them are losers." I told him something that I used to hear older people say when I was young that I didn't quite understand at the time. I said, "Son, water has a way of seeking its own level." Losers hang out with losers. Drunks hang out with drunks. Coke heads keep company with coke heads. Gossipers talk with gossipers. Those with little minds befriend each other.

Sometimes in life we have to choose between our so-called friends and our souls, between our so-called friends and our family, between our so-called friends and those who love us the most. True friends encourage us to do the right thing, and if a crowd is not supportive of our efforts to get clean and stay clean, to get sober and stay sober; if a crowd is not supportive of our efforts to get an education, expand our knowledge or improve ourselves, then the persons in that crowd, no matter what we've done with them in the past or how long we've known them, are not our friends. True friends want what is best for us. Even if they choose to remain behind, true friends will encourage us to do what is best for us.

If you don't remember anything else in this message, remember this: Take heed of the crowd with which you associate. Young man, young woman, married woman, married man, single man, and single woman—you may get lonely and discouraged sometimes, but still take heed of the crowd with which you associate.

Jesus was in the midst of a crowd that was rubbing up against him, bumping him, and touching him in any number of ways, when all of a sudden he stopped and asked, "Who touched my garments?" Those physically closest to him were baffled by this question and said, "You see the crowd pressing around you, and yet you say, 'Who touched me?' " Unknown to any of those around him, a woman who had been hemorrhaging for twelve years and who had spent all she had trying to find a cure to no avail had come up behind him in the crowd and had touched the fringes of his garment. She had said to herself, "If I touch even his garments, I shall be made whole."

One would think that such a faith came by seeing the works of Jesus or hearing the promise of his words for herself. However, according to the Scripture, this woman had only heard reports about Jesus. There is the possibility that she had never seen Jesus heal anyone. However, she was prepared to believe based upon what she had heard. We do not know how she received the reports concerning Jesus. However, somebody had to bring to her the good news about Jesus' mighty power.

We must never underestimate our importance as individual believers in spreading the gospel. The faith is carried not simply by spellbinding preachers and traveling evangelists, but by individual believers who are unashamed and enthusiastic about sharing the good news about their salvation. How do we win souls for Christ? By simply telling people what Jesus means to us. We do not win souls by debating or arguing them into the kingdom. We do not win souls by badgering and worrying them into the kingdom. We do not win souls by trying to answer questions about God, the Bible, or our religion that we don't understand ourselves. We don't win souls with fake piety and super holiness and religiosity. We don't even win souls by bragging about our church, the preacher, or the choirs.

We win souls to Christ by telling others in language that is plain and simple about what Jesus means to us. As a preacher whose vocation as well as highest joy is to help bring souls into the kingdom, I've discovered that I'm most effective not when I tell people about what Jesus did for Paul and Peter, but when I let them know what he's done for me and what he means to me. When I talk about what Jesus has done for others, I am relating what's in my head and what my mind believes. But when I talk about what Jesus means to me, I am relating what's in my heart, what my life really knows, and what my own experiences can testify to.

What I've said about myself is true for every other believer. If you want to win others to Christ, tell them what's in your heart. Tell them about what Jesus means to you personally. Your words don't have to be big; your vocabulary doesn't have to be impressive; and your knowledge of the Bible doesn't need to be great. But if what you say truly comes from your heart, then people can tell and feel it. How you say what it is you believe, sometimes more than what you say about what you believe, is what inspires others to try Jesus. There will always be persons who know more Scripture and who can quote it better than you. There will always be persons who can outdebate and outargue you. But nobody but nobody will know more than you about what the Lord has done for you.

The woman in our text had suffered a long time, and over the years her condition had continued to deteriorate. Do you know how discouraging it can be to labor with a problem and have things go from bad to worse? How frustrating it is to pray over children and then watch them go from bad to worse. How vexing it is to try to work out the problems of a relationship and see things go from bad to worse. How depressing it is to go from doctor to doctor, spend dollar after dollar, take prescription after prescription, try treatment after treatment, and watch our health go from bad to worse.

Who is to say that after suffering for twelve years this woman was not ready to give up? Yet at that very moment she either overheard somebody talking or someone told her directly about a healing prophet from Galilee. And this news so rekindled her hope that she dared to venture into the crowd and risk possible rebuff to seek out Jesus. She had no idea how he would respond to her, but based upon what she had heard, she dared to believe.

What you have to say may be the very thing the person to whom you are speaking needs to hear at that very moment. That person may be so discouraged in spirit that he or she is at the breaking point. He may be considering suicide or on the verge of a mental breakdown. She may be ready to take another drink or ready for a quick fix. He may be just plain ready to give up. Perhaps what she needs to hear at that point in her life is your testimony that, "When I was sick, God's power healed me. When I was down, God's love lifted me. When I was lost, God's mercy found me. When I was bound, the power of Jesus' redeeming love freed me. When I didn't know how I was going to make it, the Lord stepped in and made a way out of no way." Your word—not the preacher's or somebody else's that you consider to be better equipped than you—may be what some distressed and embattled soul needs to hear that will motivate him or her to search out Jesus and reach for him with such power that he pauses to ask, "Who touched me?"

What was there in the woman's touch that caused Jesus to pause? What does it mean to rub Jesus the right way? First, hers was a crowd-defying and determined touch. Her condition meant that she was ceremonially unclean and, as such, even the temple was off limits to her. She was shut off from the place that could give her the hope that she needed. Illness is bad enough, but when there is a stigma attached to it, there is a double cross to bear. Trouble plus isolation and loneliness is a doubly bitter pill to swallow. When those we would expect to support us pull away from us and shun us, the pain of our affliction cuts like a two-edged sword. Any burden is especially torturous when we have to bear it by ourselves, when people are ashamed or afraid to admit that they know us.

Sometimes as the people of God, we shut others off from the house of God by our attitudes. Our attitude about certain illnesses, certain kinds of trouble, and certain weaknesses (forgetting that all have sinned and fallen short of the glory of God); our attitudes about how people look or dress or how they talk; our attitudes about people's backgrounds or their past mistakes—these attitudes sometimes make others feel shut out and isolated from the very place where they can receive help. We who have clothing and shelter, food and family, a job and education, looks and health, still need to hear a word from the Lord because of the problems that arise in our lives. Then think about how much more a word from the Lord is needed by others—those who are hungry, homeless, and hopeless; those who are ill-clothed with broken health, no work, and no money; those who are angry or hurt or just feel downright no good. They need to hear the news that Jesus saves from the guttermost to the uttermost.

This woman with her stigmatizing bleeding condition, in the opinion of some persons, should not have even been out in public mixing with the crowd. How would people react to her if they noticed her pale emaciated body in their midst? However, for the opportunity of being blessed and healed by Jesus, this woman was prepared to defy the crowd. Whether the crowd approved of her presence or not, she was not going to miss out on her blessing. Jesus is always deeply touched, even by the simplest touch, when faith is determined to defy the crowd and press its way to victory. It must not have been easy for this frail woman to press her way through the crowd to reach Jesus, yet she was determined to make contact with the Savior. Jesus always pauses when his children don't allow obstacles and hindrances and disappointments to stop them from reaching him, when despite disappointments in the past and discouragement in the present, they press on anyhow.

At this very moment somebody needs to reach out for salvation. Somebody who has strayed needs to find the way back to God. Somebody who has been discouraged, somebody who has stopped working in the church or who has started to hold back because he or she has been hurt—this person needs to make a new commitment. At this very moment Jesus is passing by, and we can't let others stop us from reaching out to touch him. He has the healing of heart, hurt, and body; he has the hope and the help, the forgiveness and the cleansing that we need. We have to be prepared to say, "Whether I'm accepted by a certain crowd or not, I'm still coming to church. I'm still going to serve the Lord. I'm still going to work. I'm still going to shout."

This lady had a daring faith. To believe that only a touch can bring healing is a bold and daring proposition. Jesus always pauses in the presence of a daring faith. It takes a daring faith to tithe when bills are going up and real income is going down. It takes a daring faith to believe that no matter how long we've labored with our affliction or addiction or problem, we can still be delivered and healed. When the divorce rate is as high as it is, it takes a daring faith to believe that our relationship can work. When there are so many temptations and distractions, it takes a daring faith to say, "I'm going to live single and holy."

What happens when a crowd-defying, determined, and daring faith meets a powerful and sensitive Savior? Healing happens and wholeness is given; salvation comes and Jesus pauses to ask, "Who touched me?" The woman came forth and fell at Jesus' feet and told her story. Jesus looked at her and said, "Daughter, your faith has made you well; go in peace, and be healed of your disease."

He called her "daughter." She who had been cast off and shut off was called "daughter" by the Savior. We dare to defy the crowd and reach out and touch the Lord because we are one of God's children. The world may write us off, and even the crowd around the church may shun us, but we are still God's children. Who touched me? Jesus, one of your children has touched you. One of your lonely, needy, desperate, rejected, discouraged, weak, and broken children has touched you.

7

Salome:
A Mother and Jesus

Matthew 20:20–23
Suzan D. Johnson Cook

Then the mother of the sons of Zebedee came up to him, with her sons, and kneeling before him she asked him for something. And he said to her, "What do you want?" She said to him, "Command that these two sons of mine may sit, one at your right hand and one at your left, in your kingdom." But Jesus answered, "You do not know what you are asking. Are you able to drink the cup that I am to drink?" They said to him, "We are able." He said to them, "You will drink my cup, but to sit at my right and at my left is not mine to grant, but it is for those for whom it has been prepared by my Father" (Matthew 20:20 – 23).

According to the Scripture, as Jesus traveled during the three years of his ministry, he ministered to many, but little is said about those who ministered to him. It is important in the life of any servant to have devoted and loyal followers who see to his or her personal needs. Many women ministered to Jesus. Most often they were in the background of recorded Scripture, but as we examine closely, they were in the foreground of Jesus' work.

One of the women who ministered to Jesus was Salome, wife of Zebedee, the Galilean fisherman. Two of their sons were called by Jesus to become his followers, so both parents had to adjust from what they thought would be the ordinary fisherman's family to a family that would learn to be fishers of men (and women).

Salome is also believed to have been the sister of the mother of Jesus, Mary, and would therefore have been his aunt. On many occasions she was there with Jesus. Sometimes she was just supportive, not calling much attention to herself, but just there as one in the crowd. No doubt she was there to hear about the transfiguration and marveled at what God could do. I wonder how she felt when she witnessed the demons being cast out of her friend Mary Magdalene. I am almost certain that she was there to hear Jesus preach the Sermon on the Mount, and perhaps it was then that she listened to the Beatitudes or learned the prayer he taught his disciples. She had become excited about this ministry that offered possibilities of new life to those who would follow and believe.

But no matter what else she had witnessed or where she had been with him, Salome is most often remembered because of an important story about her special conversation with Jesus, which is recorded in the Gospel of Matthew. It is a powerfully moving portrait of not only a woman's relationship with Jesus but also a mother's love for her sons. There is a special connection between mothers and sons. All throughout my life I have noticed the tremendous bond that usually develops between them. Even within my own family, there is a special connection between my brother and his mother, grandmother, and aunts.

As the scene opens, Jesus had just foretold his death and also a vision for his glory. Many were moved by the passion with which it was told, perhaps to the point of speechlessness and even tears. Thus, a range of emotions was prompted. And now, this woman, who had been relatively quiet behind the scenes, was moved to make a request of the Lord because she felt privy to the inside story. Remember, Salome was part of the inside crowd who moved with and surrounded Jesus, a crowd that included her sons, James and John; Peter; and Mary, the mother of Jesus. It always amazes me how emotions and reactions can change when one thinks he or she is on the "inside." Church members who were once quiet, and whom one would think would make great leaders, suddenly can alter their personalities at the thought of becoming "close" to those they think are influential.

Salome, who felt extremely close to Jesus' personal thoughts and actions, moved in with a request, asking for Jesus to use both his personal and familial connections to provide special places for her sons, so that James and John would be able to sit preferentially on the right and left sides of him when he entered the kingdom about which he just told them. She was so caught up in what she perceived to be "glorious" that she missed entirely the point of what was to come. Perhaps she had not given thought and prayer to the fact that at a young age, Jesus had had to explain to his own earthly parents how he could no longer do what they expected of him, for he had to be about his "Father's business." Didn't she listen when Jesus preached and let them know that he and his Father were *one*, connected?

Maybe she misunderstood, but he, the Lamb of God who would take away the sins of the world, was about to be sacrificed. And in doing so, he would be the victim of a most cruel death, one that would change the course of history forevermore, one that would save his believers from their sins.

Nepotism and favoritism were her ulterior motives. She clearly presented her not-so-hidden agenda. Yet God demonstrated that God's kingdom has room for neither, for one's future belongs to God, and the outcome is not contingent upon one's family or personal connections and network. God decides who is worthy to enter, and God is no respecter of persons.

It is here that we are not only introduced to Jesus, the Savior, but are also shown the One who by his very being, presence, and existence, diplomatically and authentically disciplines as he teaches us lessons we need to know.

Only one such as Jesus could so powerfully move upon the lives of those actually present (Salome, her sons, and other disciples) while at the same time minister to those attempting to be modern-day followers. The message to us today is as thought-provoking and captivating as it was to those followers many years ago. For Jesus' response shows us that not only were favoritism and nepotism not acceptable nor tolerated in the kingdom, but also that there are clearly times when God refuses our requests.

In prayer, many of us ask for what *we* believe to be our needs and desires, rather than asking for God's will to be done in our lives. And even if God were to grant our wishes, in most cases those things that we request are more than we are able to handle. God, knowing our circumstances not only in the present but also in the future, understands what we are capable of dealing with. And there are clearly times that God says no! But the no did not come without explanation to both Salome and the sons who probably urged their mother to speak in their behalf. Jesus not only responded with a surprising negative but also informed them of the suffering that must accompany one who would bear the cup. They were asking according to their own will. God's will was that Jesus would bear the cup. The cup represented the ultimate suffering, the bearing of the burdens of many. Its contents would be the sins of the world, and only one Lamb of God (as John proclaimed) would be able to take away the world's sins. Only one Son was lifted up by God—the One with whom God was well pleased.

Yet, in their naiveté, their ambitiousness, their desire for unearned favor, Salome and her sons were brought to the understanding that they were not prepared for what it was they thought they wanted.

How often do we try to place ourselves where we are not capable of going? I often look back on times in my life when God said no. Now, at a new time and place and at a different level of understanding and maturity, it is much easier to see that God's answer in the negative was a way of protecting me in some cases and preparing me in others.

Had Jesus not said no to Salome, perhaps she would have missed the cross, which was critical to her salvation and ours as well. Had he not said no, she might have missed God's yes when she accompanied the other women to the tomb and saw that the stone was rolled away. Salome was able on that day to bring her spices to anoint the Lord's body for burial, but, praise God, he had already drunk from the cup—so that not only her sons would find a place in God's kingdom but also all daughters and sons who are daring enough to wait on the Lord and be of good courage.

8

Salome:
When the Lord Says No

Matthew 20:20–23
William D. Watley

Faith is only faith when it has learned to accept the nos as well as the yeses of God. This was a lesson that all of the disciples who walked with Jesus had to learn. This was a lesson that Paul, who counted all things as lost for the sake of Christ, had to learn. This was a lesson that Jesus learned as he agonized in the Garden of Gethsemane about the necessity of the cross. This is a lesson that each of us must learn if we intend to follow Jesus to the end.

A number of years ago I pastored a small church in which there was a large family that served as the backbone of the congregation. The mother of this family was affectionately called the "mother of the church," and most of her natural and foster children were involved in the life of that congregation. She had one son, however, who never attended church. He was not a bad young man; he never caused trouble at home or in school. He was never involved in any altercations with the police. He was a quiet and polite youngster; he just never attended church. When I asked his mother about him, she told me that, like her other children, he had been raised in the church. However, his father had become ill, and this youngster had prayed that God would heal him. When this young man's prayers were not answered in the way that he desired, he was deeply disappointed and hurt. His attitude toward God and religion soured, and he stopped attending church. I asked her to clarify her statement, since her husband was in relative good health and was attending church every Sunday. She explained to me that her son had wanted his father to be the same after his attack as he had been before, with no diminished strength or health. Her son stopped believing in God because his prayer was not answered in the precise way that he desired. Faith cannot survive unless it learns the nos as well as the yeses of God.

This was a lesson that Salome had to learn on her own faith journey. Salome has the distinction of being the only woman in the Gospels whose request was denied by Jesus. In the Gospels, whenever a woman made a request of Jesus, he usually complied. When Jesus' mother asked him to intercede for a young couple whose wine had run out at their wedding feast, he complied. He may have been irked because his mother was disregarding his timetable, but he did what she asked nevertheless. When Martha and Mary sent for him to come see about their brother Lazarus, he came. He may have been late according to their standards, but he came nevertheless. When the Syrophoenician woman brought her sick daughter to him to be healed, he granted her request. His first response may have seemed cold, but he did what she wanted nonetheless. When mothers brought young children to Jesus to bless them, he did so despite the misguided efforts of his well-intentioned disciples to shield him from those who might have disturbed him. When the woman with the issue of blood touched his garment to be healed, Jesus responded to her unspoken request and ameliorated her condition. In the Gospels, whatever women sought from the Lord they usually received. Yet he turned down the request of Salome.

Jesus' no to Salome is significant when one considers who she was. The Gospel of Matthew identifies her as one of the women, along with Mary Magdalene, who had followed Jesus from Galilee and had ministered to him. Thus, she was one of his loyal supporters and as the wife of Zebedee, who owned a flourishing fishing business, she was undoubtedly one of his strong financial backers. There is a tradition that believes Salome was the sister of Mary, Jesus' mother; if that is true, then she was Jesus' aunt. As his aunt, she had probably known him all of his life; she may have even cared for him when he was an infant. Thus, when she spoke, she did so from the perspective of strong and close family ties. Whether she was actually Jesus' aunt or not, she was, in fact, the mother of James and John, two of the Lord's closest and most prominent disciples. We naturally tend to feel close to the parents or relatives of our best friends and closest companions. Thus, when Salome spoke, she did so from the perspective of strong personal ties of friendship. Salome was one of the Lord's loyal supporters; she may have been his aunt; she was the mother of two of his closest friends; she was a person with political and personal clout among the disciples—yet Jesus told her no.

The response of Jesus is significant when one looks at the way in which she came to Jesus. According to Scripture, she knelt before him; she came humbly. She didn't come to Jesus demanding anything because she was one of his supporters. She didn't come to Jesus claiming any rights due her because she was his senior. She didn't come trying to lay any guilt trip on the Master because she was his aunt or because he had deprived her of the two sons who one day might be needed to take care of her. She came to him humbly; she came with the right attitude and spirit— yet Jesus told her no.

The response of Jesus is significant when one considers the nature of her request. Essentially she was not asking anything for herself; she was interceding for others. Her request reflected the spirit of Christ, who was always giving. We often talk about the cost of discipleship and what is required of us to be Christians. We often refer to the fact that we are called to take up crosses. However, let us not forget that Jesus is essentially a giver. He gives much more than he receives and returns much more than he keeps. When he asks for something, he does so, not to receive, but that *we* might be blessed even as we give. With all of the charges and accusations that the enemies of Jesus brought against him, no one accused him of taking or keeping anything for himself. Whatever he received he gave back to them. When he received a little boy's lunch, he gave back a banquet for five thousand persons. When he received words of praise, he gave them back as praise to his heavenly Father. When he received bread and wine, he gave it to his disciples as symbols of their redemption.

Jesus was essentially a giver and so was Salome. She gave her time to minister to Jesus and her sons to be his disciples. Her husband, Zebedee, was not getting any younger. She could have resisted the call of James and John to become disciples of Jesus. She could have asked them, "Who will take care of the family business and look after me if the two of you follow your poor cousin, Jesus, or that young vagabond prophet from Nazareth?" She may have had her own dreams regarding the careers of her sons. Salome, however, did not put any hindrance in the way of her sons' calling but became a follower of Jesus herself. She gave of her substance, and she gave of the most prized possession that any true mother has—she gave her sons to Jesus. Salome, who had been so unselfish, so loving, and so giving, only made one request of Jesus—yet he told her no.

On bended knees with her two sons she came to him and said, "Master, I have something to ask of you for these two sons of mine who are already close to you and whom you have already taken into your confidence on more than one occasion. Command that one may sit on your right hand and the other on your left."

Now before we criticize Salome for her request, let us observe that there is nothing wrong *per se* with a mother looking out for the best interests of her children. What good parent doesn't want a better life for his or her children? Good parents are not envious of their children's successes. Good parents hope that their children will go further in life than they have, and if they can do anything to pave the way to help them, they will. Salome in her request was only looking out for the well-being of her children as any good mother should—yet Jesus told her no.

Let us further note that there is nothing wrong *per se* with the desire to be next to Jesus in the kingdom that he will establish. Salome and her sons are to be commended for believing in the power of this homeless, penniless, weaponless, armyless preacher of God's word whom they followed to bring a kingdom into being. Their request showed an audacious leap of faith. Some mothers want their sons to be seated next to the Caesars of history; others want their sons seated next to persons of great social standing and wealth. But Salome desired that her sons be seated next to Jesus.

I once knew a sainted lady who earnestly desired that her son become a preacher. Soon after I started preaching, she told me how much she wanted her son to preach. The young man, who was standing next to her said, "Mama, I don't mind preaching. I just never received the call." There is nothing wrong *per se* with a request to be next to Jesus— yet our Lord told Salome no.

Jesus recognized that although Salome's faith was well intentioned, it had much to learn. He said: "You don't know what you are asking. Are you able to drink the cup that I am to drink?" They said to him, "We are able." He said to them, "You will drink my cup, but to sit at my right hand and my left hand is not mine to grant; it is for those for whom it has been prepared."

Before we can fully enter the kingdom, there are some cups from which faith must drink, some of which can be bitter. Our inclination is to ask God to remove the bitter cups from our lives. Sometimes God says no to us because those cups qualify us to enter the kingdom of God. I once knew a lady of great faith who constantly prayed for healing. Her healing never came, but she had such a sweet disposition and such faith that she encouraged everyone who met her. I don't deny that her cup was bitter, but the fact that she drank it well allowed her to enter into the kingdom.

It is said that a monk prayed that he might have the marks of the Lord upon his hands and feet. He had a dream in which he saw a mark on the Lord's body that the world had forgotten. It was the mark upon his shoulder made by the cross as he bore it to Calvary. The monk discovered that he could only have the marks of the Lord on his hands and feet if he had the marks on the shoulder that come from bearing the cross.

If we do not drink of certain cups, then we lose the key to the kingdom for which our faith unlocks the door. If we do not drink from certain cups, then we cancel our reservations on the journey that leads from earth to heaven and from time to eternity. If we do not drink from certain cups, then we cease going from strength to strength and from glory to glory.

It is only as we drink from certain cups that we enter the kingdom. It was only as Charlotte Elliot drank from the cup of illness that she wrote her hymn of commitment, "Just As I Am, Without One Plea." It was only as Charles Wesley drank from the cup of persecution that he wrote "Jesus, Lover of My Soul." It was only as a sick pastor drank from the cup of forced retirement that he wrote "Abide with Me." It was only as John Newton drank from the cup of remorse over his involvement in slavery and the wonder of salvation that he wrote "Amazing Grace." It was only as a pastor and his sick wife drank from the cup of painful separation as he did the Lord's work that they wrote "God Will Take Care of You." It was only as Fanny Crosby drank from the cup of blindness that she wrote "Blessed Assurance"; "Close to Thee"; "Saviour, More Than Life to Me"; "Pass Me Not"; and "I Am Thine, O Lord."

It was only as Elisha Hoffman drank from the cup of ministering to the distressed and brokenhearted that he wrote "I Must Tell Jesus." It was only as blind George Matheson drank from the cup of a jilted lover that he wrote "O Love That Will Not Let Me Go." It was only after Thomas Dorsey drank from the cup of sorrow as he mourned the passing of his wife that he wrote "Precious Lord, Take My Hand." It was only as black people drank from the cup of slavery that the spirituals were born. As they drank they sang "I'm So Glad Trouble Don't Last Always." I repeat: It is only as we drink from certain cups that we enter the kingdom.

Perhaps Jesus gave Salome a further explanation: "You and your sons shall drink of my cup. James will be among the first of my disciples to be martyred for the cause of the kingdom. John will live to be an old man, but he shall experience persecution, banishment, and distress. He will see all of his companions die one by one until in extreme old age he will be left alone with nothing to comfort him but the memory of vanished years and the hope of an eternal future. As their mother and as a loyal follower, you will have your share of the cup of sorrow, but I still must say no to your request. To sit at my right hand and my left hand is not mine to grant, but it is for those for whom it has been prepared by my Father."

Jesus could have added: "If I say yes to you, I'll have to say no to too many people. If I say yes to you, I'll have to say no to too many Christians who will come after you, who will face raging lions and be burned at the stake, and who have as much right to those places as you. If I say yes to you, I'll have to say no to martyrs such as John Wycliffe, Joan of Arc, and the many missionaries who will carry my gospel to regions unknown. If I say yes to you, I'll have to say no to faithful men and women who will stand by the church for years, who will struggle to keep the doors open in lean times. If I say yes to you, I'll have to say no to too many oppressed black people who will die with a heaven in their view."

Sometimes God says no to us so that he can say yes to others. Many a Christian has stayed beside the sickbed of someone, praying for recovery in this life. But while God said no to the one who was praying, God said yes to the one who was sick. God told that person, "Yes, you've fought a good fight; you've run a good race; you deserve your reward. Come, blessed of my Father, receive the kingdom prepared for you from the foundation of the world." Several years ago God said no to me, but yes to my father—"Come on home."

I'm glad Jesus said no to Salome because then he was able to say yes to another host. John, called the Revelator, wrote about it:

After this I looked, and behold, a great multitude which no man could number, from every nation, from all tribes and peoples and tongues, standing before the throne and before the Lamb, clothed in white robes, with palm branches in their hands, and crying out with a loud voice, "Salvation belongs to our God who sits upon the throne, and to the Lamb!" . . . Then one of the elders addressed me, saying, "Who are these, clothed in white robes, and whence have they come?" I said to him, "Sir, you know." And he said to me, "These are they who have come out of the great tribulation; they have washed their robes and made them white in the blood of the Lamb.

Therefore are they before the throne of God,
    and serve him day and night within his temple;
    and he who sits upon the throne will shelter them with
      his presence.
They shall hunger no more, neither thirst any more;
. . .
For the Lamb in the midst of the throne will be their
    shepherd,
    and he will guide them to springs of living water;
and God will wipe away every tear from their eyes."
                —Revelation 7:9 – 10; 13 – 17, RSV

9

Martha:
The One Thing That Is Necessary

Luke 10:38–42
Suzan D. Johnson Cook

Now as they went on their way, he entered a village; and a woman named Martha received him into her house. And she had a sister called Mary, who sat at the Lord's feet and listened to his teaching. But Martha was distracted with much serving and she went to him and said, "Lord, do you not care that my sister has left me to serve alone? Tell her then to help me."

But the Lord answered her, "Martha, Martha, you are anxious and troubled about many things; one thing is needful. Mary has chosen the good portion, which shall not be taken away from her" (Luke 10:38 – 42).

It is good for us to know that in the busy ministry of Jesus the Christ, there were those times and places where he could find a place called home and people called friends. Throughout his ministry these places and people were few and far between. Therefore, when we come to those times that are intimate and sensitive, we call particular attention to them and we cherish them. As one who is active in the ministry, I know how infrequently one finds solace and a resting place. Those places, people, times, and circumstances that allow me to just be myself, where I am able to place my feet under a table of love, are longed for and greatly appreciated when they arise. One place in particular for me was the home of "Ma Bert," a special woman in Cambridge, Massachusetts, who always invited those of us in college and church together to her home for Sunday dinner.

Jesus, too, found such a home in Bethany, with three

whom he had grown to love and for whom he had great admiration and affection. The two women in this household were named Mary and Martha. Martha was more the homemaker type. She enjoyed, it seemed, having nice warm meals prepared for her family as well as for their special friends who would visit. Mary, on the other hand, was more the contemplative one, who would meditate and read the Scriptures and dream and explore within her mind the various ways that the gospel could be lived out. One was busy in the preparation of food and the other household needs, while the other was more prophetic. Both were important; they were two women living in a world where Jesus was present. They were excited and were trying to understand how they best could lead lives that would reflect the teaching and the living out of this new gospel. Many believers were wrestling, praying, and grappling with this new word—"gospel." Jesus had said to them, "The time is fulfilled, and the kingdom of God is at hand; repent, and believe in the gospel" (Mark 1:15).

Martha sought to make the home as comfortable as possible for Jesus. On this particular day, Jesus was coming for a visit. It is obvious that this was not his first time there, for there were no introductory comments nor salutations, and there was a familiarity that was instantaneous. As soon as Jesus arrived, Martha, whose very name translated in the Greek and Aramaic means "lady," engaged Jesus in dialogue about some problems with the way Mary had prepared for Jesus' coming. Martha perceived that Mary had failed to make the appropriate contributions to the household. She then raised a question and gave a directive: "Lord, do you not care that my sister has left me to serve alone? Tell her then to help me." Certainly there are some traditional role expectations lined up in that question, but coupled with it is the inference that one is not worthy as a woman unless one is making contributions in the manner that Martha prescribed.

As a woman in ministry, and one whom the Lord has blessed with the office and responsibility of pastor, I immediately identified with the text. Often there are expectations from both women and men who are observing us in our various contexts, who bring their tradition of what a woman's role should be. Therefore, they immediately identify those of us who are pastors by the gender rather than the office. As one who grew up female in this society, and one who preferred being contemplative rather than busy doing the household chores, I was aware that there were suggestions that perhaps I was lazy or not living up to what society expected of me. And so, in childhood, in adulthood, as well as in pastoring, some personal and sometimes painful and very nontraditional choices had to be made because I was at a different place and point in terms of expectations and role identification.

Well, Jesus responded to both Martha's request and her cry for understanding with a compassionate lesson for Martha and for those of us who are modern-day readers and interpreters of this text.

First, there is a comparison between the different types of women with different interests and gifts. Certainly no one type is better or worse than the other, simply different. There is, no doubt, a place for the Marthas of this world, for homemakers make valuable contributions to the life of this world. Yet there is also an opportunity for those unlike Martha, those who may be less excited about the household work and prefer to contribute in other ways to the prophetic tasks that are also important to the Lord.

Jesus took this comparison one step further, for he let it be known that those who are often busy with many things, whether in the kitchen or elsewhere, may become distracted so much by the busyness and the number of things they have to juggle that they may forget the one thing that is most important to God. They may just very well forget the time necessary to reflect and learn and pray on the doing of ministry and servanthood. Mary was sitting at the feet of Jesus, where she could absorb the depths of the meaning of his work and witness and whereby she, too, could one day be one who would follow in his footsteps. Rest, reflection, and renewal are important for kingdom building.

But the third area that necessitates our drawing attention to Jesus' response is that there is always a *choice*. Martha chose to be busy with household preparations. Mary chose to sit at Jesus' feet. For in choosing one or the other, the real issue with Jesus is choosing what is really important. Is it the number of things or circumstances one chooses to participate in, or is it more important to choose the most meaningful thing, and that is a relationship with God through Jesus?

In this story Mary chose the one "good portion," for

although a banquet will fill one's stomach for a few hours or even a few days, it is not lasting. Spiritual food, however, allows one to feast for the remainder of his or her life, for one's walk with God lasts and cannot be taken away by time, persons, or the many prevailing issues that may plague us.

I remember well that when I was called to become pastor of Mariners' Temple Baptist Church, I began to sit at the feet of Jesus for literally hours and days, reflecting on all the lessons and observations I had had in my previous years in ministry. I thought about the new level of responsibility, stewardship, and trust that God was allowing me as I was moving from a youth minister in my home church to the senior pastor of a new work. There were several choices I had to make consciously, not so that others would be comfortable with me, but so that I could fulfill what I believed God's expectations of me were. Part of that choice had to do with tradition as it related to both gender and office of ministry. The Marthas of the church world would come with predetermined expectations that they would place upon me in terms of dress, cooking, serving, preaching, and the utilizing of various gifts and talents. It was then when I began to see that because there were so few role models and mentors who were female, my position was both a blessing and a burden: a burden because I would not have many women to whom I could vent my feelings or off whom I could bounce my ideas, yet a blessing because since there had been so few women in ministry, it would mean that I, with Jesus' help, could make some serious choices about who I wanted to be without a lot of baggage attached. I chose not to be bothered by those who expected my dress to be a certain length or color. I chose to use the common sense and good values and judgment that the Lord had given me to determine that I would define my own style of dress, which would be comfortable yet not offensive to those whom I deemed important and to whom I was accountable.

I also made a conscious choice not to go into the kitchen every time the church was having a social function. Yes, I would make my contributions to the community, but I also would make it clear that women's contributions were not limited to the kitchen. There had to be a decision about how I would choose to function in my office as a pastor, regardless of gender.

Still, there were other choices that had to be made,

some that ministers continue to grapple with. Those of us who are musically gifted and talented have to choose in our new places how best we can empower people in our ministries. Should we, every time a musician does not show, run over to the piano and play our favorite hymn? I chose not to, thus allowing others with gifts to utilize them and also increasing the awareness of the importance of a strong music ministry.

Jesus' response to Martha hit home in an incredible way, for I believe that I am one of the Marys of this life—one who has made a conscious, yet sometimes very nontraditional effort to sit at Jesus' feet and be prophetic.

There is certainly a place for all of us in this world, the Marys and the Marthas, and still others who fall somewhere between the two. But what is most important is that we who are Christian make sure we choose what is most important to God—that good part which lives on forever, that walks with God, in helping the Word to be flesh and dwell amongst us.

10

Martha:
When Faith Becomes Frustrated

Luke 10:38–42
William D. Watley

No matter how much we love Jesus, how sincere we are in our service, or how much of our selves and our substance we are willing to give, there are times when our faith becomes frustrated. Our text recounts such a time in the relationship between Jesus and two of his closest friends and most loyal supporters, Martha and Mary of the village of Bethany. These two sisters truly loved Jesus, and I believe that he sincerely loved them. An interesting feature of the Gospels is that no mention is ever made of a visit by Jesus to the homes of his own sisters and brothers. There is evidence in the Gospels that Jesus' own brothers and sisters did not affirm his ministry during his lifetime. They seemed to have been chagrined by it and at one time sought to restrain him because they thought he had suffered from a mental or emotional breakdown. The reaction of Jesus' own flesh and blood to his ministry must have been disappointing and painful to him. We are usually hurt when we are not supported by our own families—by those who are bone of our bone and flesh of our flesh. We are usually discouraged when we must look outside of our household and family for affirmation and encouragement in those things that really matter to us.

When one reads the Gospels, one gets the impression that Martha and Mary were like sisters to Jesus and that their brother Lazarus was like another brother. Although Jesus said, "Foxes have holes, and birds of the air have nests; but the Son of man has nowhere to lay his head" (Matthew 8:20), he did not make that statement in the village of Bethany. Whenever he came to Bethany, Jesus knew that there was a home whose doors swung open in welcome to receive him and friends who were like family to him. At this point in his ministry, cynics and scoffers, disbelievers and discreditors criticized everything he said and every move he made. The enemies of the truth that he was and that he taught were constantly seeking ways to entrap him so that they could undermine his ministry and destroy his movement. Living in a fishbowl is a difficult thing to do. Candidates for political office, movie stars, athletes, and other well-known personalities have all discovered that living under the constant scrutiny and glare of the public is a demanding and sometimes demeaning lifestyle. "It ain't easy" when everything one says or does is examined, weighed, and evaluated. "It ain't easy" when one is aware that there are those standing on the sidelines waiting and wishing for one to stumble. As many preachers and others who have been rightly or wrongly put on some kind of moral pedestal have discovered, life in the spotlight before the public, although glamorous, can also be very lonely.

All of us whose lives are constantly being criticized by the public need a shelter from the stormy blast. We need companions with whom we can dare be ourselves. We need someplace where we can relax. All of us need friends with whom we don't have to be political or weigh every word; friends whom we can trust and who have no hidden agenda. Sometimes on the job we resent the boss's friends, and sometimes in church we resent the pastor's friends. We must never become so small that we begrudge others their friends. Everyone has a right to have them and everybody needs them. Jesus needed them and so do the rest of us. We all need others who, beyond their official capacity, love us just for ourselves. I believe that even if Jesus had not been the Son of God incarnate, Martha, Mary, and Lazarus would still have been his friends. We can imagine how much of a comfort they were to him. All of us know the joy of being able to go into warm surroundings and shut out the pressures and tensions of the outside world and be with those whom we love and who love us simply for ourselves.

Whenever Jesus went to the home of Martha, Mary, and Lazarus, it was a special time for each of them. Martha was sensitive to the pressures that her friend was under and was concerned that everything go just right whenever Jesus was there. Martha was one of those properly organized homemakers who believe that everything has a place and everything should be kept in its place. Although her house was organized and neat, it was still warm and cozy and looked lived in. Martha took pride in her ability as a homemaker, and whenever she entertained, she did it with style. Whatever God's children do, we should do with pride and with style. Whether we are pushing a broom, cooking a dish, or serving a table, we should take pride in the task. Whatever we do represents not only us but also the God who made us, and God does not make junk. Whatever we do should be done in such a manner that people are aware that they are in the presence of one of God's redeemed children.

On this day, however, things were not going well for Martha in the kitchen. She had scorched the rice, burned the cornbread, and grease had splattered on her as she was frying the chicken. On this Palestinian day, with all of the serious cooking and moving around that she was doing, the kitchen became unusually hot and so did she. In her haste she had even dropped one of her favorite bowls. She was simply trying to do too much. "Where," she asked, "is my sister Mary?" She looked into the living room, and there sat Mary, prim and proper, with admiring eyes and a pleasant smile at the feet of Jesus. At first Martha shook her head in disgust, sighed, and went back to her work. She was preparing three meats—chicken, beef, and lamb—the salad had to be tossed, the cake iced, and some finishing touches had to be added to the table setting. She had too much to do to argue with Mary, and besides, she didn't want to disturb Jesus.

However, as Martha went back to her work, all she could think about was Mary, her younger and prettier sister, sitting at Jesus' feet. To add insult to injury, it occurred to her that Jesus knew she was in the kitchen by herself and that he wasn't sensitive enough to suggest that Mary help her. It just seemed to Martha that while she was doing all of the work, Mary was receiving all of the attention from Jesus. Finally, when her thoughts got the best of her, she wiped her hands on her apron, strode into the living room with her hands on her hips, looked at Jesus and said: "Lord, do you not care that my sister has left me to serve alone? Tell her then to help me."

Let me hastily observe that when I look at this passage, it seems to me that since the beginning, our faith tradition has been plagued by problems in the kitchen. Some of the biggest arguments in the church occur in and around the kitchen. If today we must contend with problems in the kitchen, at least we can take comfort in the fact that Jesus had to deal with the same things.

Let it be understood that Martha did not mind serving Jesus. That was her talent and she gladly gave it; that was her way of expressing love, devotion, and commitment, and so she had served without complaint. Her service was not like that which is rendered by so many of us who will give ourselves but complain while we're doing it. There are some people who have the ability and even the desire to serve, but one has to go through so much trouble to get them to do anything, that it's easier to simply leave them alone. Some people must be begged and coddled and their egos and feelings must be constantly stroked before they consent to function. Others will work, but they are so disagreeable, and they grumble so much and cause so much confusion that we regret ever having asked them. Martha wasn't like that; she enjoyed serving and made her service a joy for others. Thus, her conduct in this instance was out of character. She had reached one of those moments in her faith journey where she had become frustrated as she tried as best she could to serve Jesus.

All of us at times become frustrated in our service—in our efforts to give our all and do our best with a sincere heart and willing spirit. Frustrated faith is faith that is out of character, and all of us can act out of character on occasion. When faith becomes frustrated, we become irritable, short-tempered, and likely to snap at others. When faith becomes frustrated, labors of love become burdens, and we feel exploited, oppressed, and taken advantage of, when ordinarily we would have felt honored or privileged to be asked to serve. Frustrated faith engenders attitudes, personalities, and spirits that are evil, mean, ungodly, and beneath what is expected from God's children. When faith becomes frustrated, we lose the joy from what usually gives us joy. If some of us have lost the joy of serving, singing, preaching, or living, maybe our problem is a severe case of frustrated faith.

Martha became frustrated in her service because she felt that while she did all the work, Mary received all of the attention. Faith becomes frustrated when we feel that while we do the work, others receive the recognition. Faith becomes frustrated when we have attended meeting after meeting throughout the year, tried to participate faithfully in all the activities of an organization, struggled to carry the financial weight, and then have had to watch as others, who haven't done as much, attended as often, or given as much, are put on the program and are up front and out front receiving recognition. Faith becomes frustrated when on the annual day, people who haven't attended much of anything are the first to jump in line for the processional with their new outfits. Faith becomes frustrated when committees are recognized and people who haven't attended one meeting or done a dime's worth of work are the first to stand up with their chests out as if they have done it all. Faith becomes frustrated when we have been sweating in the kitchen, sweating in choir rehearsal, sweating in meetings, sweating in the board room, sweating at home because companions and children don't understand why we spend so much time and money in the church, and no one seems to be aware or paying any attention to our sacrifices and contributions.

Faith becomes frustrated when we believe that those whom we are trying to help or serve are not paying us proper attention. It's a terrible feeling to believe that those whom we're knocking ourselves out for, working and sweating for, making sacrifices for, are not appreciative of what we're doing on their behalf. We're the ones in the kitchen and in choir rehearsal; we're the ones trying to push the church program and fight off hell hounds; we're the ones who are covering the pastor's back when he or she is not around. Yet we are barely recognized because someone else who, in our opinion, is all talk and no work is grinning and getting the attention we feel should be ours. We are frustrated when we are working our fingers to the bone, and the church or the company or our companion or the children or the club doesn't seem to care. We are frustrated when we're trying to do right and give our all, and Jesus doesn't seem to care. He doesn't seem to be sensitive to what we're doing and all we're going through.

In spite of our services, it seems as if the Lord is paying more attention to someone else—some sinner who is not doing anything for God's cause. In spite of our labors, we still have problems, and so we come to God and say, "Lord, do you not care that, like Elijah, I'm down here feeling as if I'm working by myself? Do you not care that those who are supposed to be helping me have sat down and dumped the burden in my lap? Do you not care that despite the bills that

I'm struggling with, I'm trying to keep up my tithes and offerings? Do you not care that I'm being talked about and falsely accused? I asked you to do something, and you didn't say yes to my prayer. Do you not care? Tell that group that you have blessed with beautiful homes, expensive cars, fine clothes, good educations, more energy and abundant talent to come in here and help me carry this load."

Martha was frustrated because Mary was not doing what Martha wanted her to do. We can become easily frustrated when we are not able to accept the different ways others have of expressing their love for Jesus. We often want everyone to be like us, to worship like us, and to serve like us. Everyone doesn't have Martha's gifts. Consequently, everyone is not cut out for kitchen work. Sometimes Marthas become critical of Marys because they want their sisters or brothers to join them in the kitchen. What Marthas sometimes fail to understand is that Jesus' heart is big enough to receive both the adoration of Marys in the living room as well as the sweat of Marthas in the kitchen. There is room in the kingdom of God, in the church, and in the heart of Jesus for both Marthas and Marys.

We need hands like Martha's to do physical work, and we need hearts like Mary's to point us to the spiritual. We need Marthas to admonish us to be practical, and we need Marys to remind us to be faithful. We need Marthas to raise money, and we need Marys, who have also sat at the feet of Jesus, to remind us that we must raise money in ways that are consistent with what the Master has taught. We need Marthas who know how to work the plan, and we need Marys who know how to plan the work. We need Marthas in the kitchen preparing food, and we need Marys who can teach the young what they have learned as they have sat at Jesus' feet. We need Marthas to remind us that there is a time when we ought to stand up and speak, and we need Marys to remind us that there is also a time to hold our peace. When Marthas have done all they can, we need Marys to pray the program through to victory. Without Marthas the dinner would not be prepared, and without Marys we might forget whose grace makes our eating possible.

Some of us like to be all Martha—all work and not enough sitting at the feet of Jesus. Some of us like to be all Marys—all sitting at the feet of Jesus but no work. Jesus calls us to be both Mary and Martha. He not only tells us to "go," but also tells us to "come apart" and pray. He not only takes us to the mount of Transfiguration, but also takes us to the valley where a sick boy is in need of healing. He not only tells us to go into all the world and make disciples of all nations, but also tells us to tarry in Jerusalem until we receive power from on high. He not only leads us to the upper room to worship and to the Garden of Gethsemane to pray, but also points us to Calvary to give our all. As Marthas our hands are prepared to anoint his dead body, but as Marys we end up at his feet worshiping our resurrected Lord.

In the Gospel of John we read of another dinner in Martha's home in Bethany. The occasion was the celebration of Lazarus being raised from the dead by Jesus. As usual, Martha was in the kitchen serving, and Mary was sitting at the feet of Jesus. The dinner was larger, and there was more work to be done. However, this time there was no complaint from Martha about Mary. They were both so full of joy, so full of Christ's peace, so full of gratitude for what Jesus had done in their lives, that they had no time to complain about each other. I don't have to frustrate you and you don't have to frustrate me; Jesus can fulfill and satisfy each of us. We can each find our good portion in Christ that cannot be taken away. Criticism can't take it away. Crises can't take it away. Not even Calvary can take it away. I've found my portion in Jesus. Have you found your portion in Jesus? Do you know for yourself that he's a Savior, a healer divine, a friend who sticks closer than a brother, a burden bearer, a problem solver, a heavy load lifter, and the resurrection and the life?

11

Mary of Bethany:
The Best She Could

John 12:1–8
Suzan D. Johnson Cook

Six days before the Passover, Jesus came to Bethany, where Lazarus was, whom Jesus had raised from the dead. There they made him a supper; Martha served, and Lazarus was one of those at table with him. Mary took a pound of costly ointment of pure nard and anointed the feet of Jesus and wiped his feet with her hair; and the house was filled with the fragrance of the ointment. But Judas Iscariot, one of his disciples (he who was to betray him), said, "Why was this ointment not sold for three hundred denarii and given to the poor?" This he said, not that he cared for the poor but because he was a thief, and as he had the money box he used to take what was put into it. Jesus said, "Let her alone, let her keep it for the day of my burial. The poor you always have with you, but you do not always have me" (John 12:1 – 8).

I guess it is just in my blood. I really love and look forward to those weekly family dinners on Sunday that have become a standing tradition in the Johnson family. No matter how many hours each of us has been at church nor how many afternoon social or religious engagements we all are involved with, on Sundays, at a designated and agreed-upon time, we collectively gather in the early evening at my mother's house. It is our opportunity to break bread together and to make our love connection. Conversations include school choices for those entering college, critiques of my Sunday morning sermon, and various other updates, observations, and dialogues. It is quite an experience and exchange, dating back, I believe, perhaps to our African ancestors. Certainly it has been practiced routinely for three generations of which I am aware. Most of our southern relatives and extended family have the same practice as well. Our guest list is not, however, limited to blood relatives, for each of us is free to invite those precious to us.

The table is immaculately set with crystal, china, and silverware. A menu prepared with love dresses the table. There are usually two or three different meats, three or four vegetables, at least two starches, homemade bread, and, to everyone's delight, a surprise dessert. All are special, but banana pudding is my favorite. But beyond the wonderful cuisine, something else, something quite significant, is also happening: the generations are interacting and learning from and sharing with one another. Even the meal itself is representative of the richness of the different generations— each recipe has been passed down through the years.

This theme of sharing one with another is common throughout many different scenarios in life. In the movie *Do the Right Thing*, the contemporary, controversial director and author Spike Lee presents the audience with a wonderfully moving scene involving the lead character's sister. She is braiding the hair of another black woman, a senior citizen, on the front steps of her home. Even though the end result is intended to be a new hairdo, the older woman shares her experienced wisdom with the younger woman, and the younger woman shares her hopes and dreams with the older woman. Dreams realized are in the presence of dreams yet to be born. It is an intergenerational exchange, where wisdom and the search for it are carefully juxtaposed. It grasped me as I paralleled it with my own family dinner and what was happening there.

In our own family exchanges there is much laughter, reminiscence, and reflection. Recently at one gathering, however, my twelve-year-old nephew began to speak. As he did, an elder relative who rarely visits was obviously perturbed by the youngster's conversation, and she rudely interrupted. Her body language seemed to suggest that he was too young to speak at this table. There was an awkward hush from those of us who normally join together, for without articulating it, we all knew something was wrong in the midst of that special happening. Someone soon remarked, "Let's give him a chance to finish; everyone here can speak." He was able to finish his thought, but he had been embarrassed, stopped, and criticized for doing nothing more than what he considered to be a good gesture and demonstration of this love for being with his family. He wanted to be an active participant rather than a quiet, by-standing observer. It is amazing how actions intended for good can often be miscommunicated.

In the Bible there is an example of a similar situation that was misconstrued. Mary of Bethany acted and served out of a love impulse but was harshly criticized for pouring her precious ointment over Jesus' feet. She had taken something most special to her, an alabaster flask of precious oil, to use as an expressive gesture as Jesus sat with his disciples. They were having a feast and sharing special moments while the Lord was present. She, too, was happy to be in Jesus' presence.

I imagine their gathering together at the home of Lazarus as Jesus' extended family included many of the same qualities as my own family's meetings. Perhaps as they reminisced on their shared events, they thought of the feeding of the multitudes, the Sermon on the Mount, or the wonderful parables Jesus had taught them. As they gathered, Mary came forward to share what she had, an alabaster flask filled with precious oil. Yet as she poured her ointment on his body and she swept his feet with her hair, the disciples did not recognize her actions as a contribution to, but rather as an intrusion upon their activity. Like my elder relative who interrupted my nephew, several disciples spoke indignantly. In other words, Mary caused quite a stir, so much so that some emotional disturbance was occurring. The disciples saw her actions as insignificant, irrelevant, and meaningless, for she had overstepped her defined and assigned role. First, they were upset by what they saw as an interruption of their private time with Jesus. Second, there was also an emotional response to what they perceived to be a loss of profit as well as a waste of good time and energy.

How often do persons impose their value systems upon others? Often church service and stewardship are viewed by those outside of the fold as waste. How often do we impose our definitions of roles and what we feel is important on others who wish to share in our experiences? It's frightful to see in my daily walk just how often others impose their demands and desires on those whom they feel are less significant. This situation can sometimes cause people to withdraw from participating in church or other activities because of low self-esteem. They have been made to feel that no matter how hard they work, there will be others who will find fault with what they have done. As another example, hundreds, and I would venture to say thousands, of children and youth have run away from home because they feel their parents won't allow them to express their feelings or desires. When the parents say they want "the best" for their kids, it often negates who the children want to be. Teenagers especially, who are trying to define themselves and find their meaning in life, are often put down as insignificant.

Church leaders who out of their own personal needs dictate the course of action rather than empower the laity to have a sense of ownership in ministry are yet another example of role confusion and treating others as insignificant. Equipping the saints for the work of the ministry requires an enormous amount of exchange and interchange, and sometimes even a sacrifice of one's own ego needs for the sake of others. How tragic it is for pastors to belittle their members, who may have limitations, but who are willing to use what they have for God's service.

Perhaps the most recurring misuse of power that stands out in my mind and life are those who see women as insignificant in the life of ministry. The expressions used are similar to those that were probably directed to Mary of Bethany—"Why are you wasting your time?"—as though they are able to define what is good and bad use of another's time. Many constantly reject the vessels that women bring to the Lord. Instead of seeing us as co-laborers who wish to share in the feast, a significant number see us as intruders into their celebration. How awful it is, at the end of the twentieth century, that sisters are still denied access to a number of ministers' conferences, pulpits, and churches. Why do people feel as though Jesus is only for them? Is not God a God of inclusiveness?

As all of the negative, rejecting, criticizing comments were directed to this woman, Jesus interrupted and pointed out the significance of her action. It was a crucial time, just before the Last Supper; and at this house where they were gathered, more than just a Passover celebration was occurring. Sacrifice and exchange were also happening. What to her was a gesture of love became preparation for his most mighty act. It reminds us of the words of the psalmist, who in Psalm 37 declared, "Commit your way to the LORD, trust in him and he will act." It also reminds us of a contemporary gospel songwriter who penned:

Just ordinary people, God uses ordinary people.
He chooses people just like me and you
who are willing to do as He commands.
God uses people that will give Him all,
no matter how small your all may seem to you;
because little becomes much as you place it
*   in the Master's hand.*[1]

Perhaps this experience of Mary of Bethany triggered a response in you. Recall examples in your own life of others who tried to demonstrate love, but whose efforts were rejected. Or if you've been the recipient of righteous indignation, know that Jesus is clearly able to distinguish the meaningfulness of your actions. Whatever resources you make available to him become useful for the work of the kingdom.

Others may not understand. In fact, many may criticize our involvement in God's service, but we know that we are the hands through which God works:

If when you give the best of your service,
Telling the world that the Savior is come;
Be not dismayed when men don't believe you;
He understands; He'll say "Well done."[2]

I thank God that the gathering of the Johnson clan each week, despite the times of uninvited conflict, provides a time of affirmation for us. We are reminded that each of us is important to one another. We realize who we are as a proud African American family, steeped deep in a tradition of love and sharing. But more importantly, as this woman in Bethany found out, we realize *whose* we are—we are part of Jesus' family.

---

[1]From "Ordinary People." Words and music by Danniebelle Hall. Copyright © 1977 Birdwing Music / Cherry Lane Music Publishing Co., Inc. (Adm. by the Sparrow Corp., P.O. Box 5010, Brentwood, TN 37024-5010) / Danniebelle Music. All rights reserved. International copyright secured. Used by permission. From the recording "Danniebelle Live" by Danniebelle Hall. The Sparrow Corporation. All rights reserved. Reprinted by special permission.

[2]From "He Understands, He'll Say 'Well Done,' " by Lucie E. Campbell.

12

Mary of Bethany: *When Love Is Criticized*

John 12:1–8
William D. Watley

Sincerity and purity of heart will not exempt our love from criticism. Actions that are unselfish, that seek to give our best and our all, will not be appreciated by everyone. Innocence and tenderheartedness do not protect us from misunderstanding. Minding our own business as we express our love toward those we care for will not shield us from faultfinders.

Mary of Bethany, the sister of Martha, is an excellent example of these truths. In all of the New Testament, Mary of Bethany is one of the most quiet, unobtrusive, and tenderhearted persons that we meet. Mary never pushed for any recognition or authority, and she never sought the spotlight. She never spoke out of turn or acted harshly, irreverently, or disrespectfully toward anyone. Although she never criticized anyone, she was criticized; and although she minded her own business and never bothered anyone, people bothered her.

Let us note that we don't have to bother anyone for people to bother us. We don't have to interfere with anyone else's business for others to interfere with ours. Sometimes we believe that if we mind our own business, stay in our corner of the world, and remain quiet, we will be unnoticed and left alone, and the trouble and the tragedies that strike the lives of others will somehow pass us by. A number of us simply desire to be left alone. A number of senior citizens or persons who have reached their declining years desire to be left alone and untouched by the many changes and upheavals that they see around them in order to spend their remaining years in peace. On our jobs and in our churches, a number of us want to be left alone so that we can work and worship without interference or hindrance from those around us. Sometimes within our own families and at home we earnestly desire a little quiet and space. We hope that those we love will love us enough to leave us alone for awhile.

Life, however, has a way of intruding upon our space. Most victims of crime are those who were not bothering anyone when they were attacked. Most of the Jews Hitler killed were not bothering anyone when they were arrested and sentenced to death. Most of those noble Africans who were brought to these shores as slaves were not bothering anyone when they were captured. We do not live in paradise or utopia. We live in a world where sin is bold enough to attack and evil is without conscience regarding those whom it seeks to destroy. Thus, one of the basic facts of life is that whether we bother others or not, we are going to be bothered. None of us will have the privilege of being left alone. Even our sincere acts of devotion and love will be criticized by those who do not understand them.

In the Gospels the spotlight falls upon Mary only three times. In no instance is she bothering anyone, and yet two of the three times she is being criticized. An interesting feature about the three instances when Mary is highlighted is that she is at Jesus' feet. In one instance she is at Jesus' feet because of a heavy heart. Lazarus, her brother, had become ill, and she and her sister, Martha, had sent word to Jesus to come to the bedside of his good friend. Jesus did not immediately respond to their request; consequently, when he arrived in Bethany, Lazarus had already been dead for four days. When Mary and Martha heard that Jesus was coming, the outspoken Martha went to meet him, while the tenderhearted Mary remained in the house. After having her faith in the Master's credibility restored, Martha went to her sister and told her that Jesus had come and was calling for her. Mary immediately went to Jesus, fell at his feet, and with words of disappointed love said, "Lord, if you had been here, my brother would not have died" (John 11:32). This is the only time that Mary was not criticized when she was at the feet of Jesus.

The other instances when Mary was at the feet of Jesus involved acts of worship and adoration and expressions of love and gratitude. These were the times that she encountered criticism. During one of his visits to Jerusalem, Jesus was in the home of Martha and Mary. Martha was in the kitchen cooking a meal, and Mary was in the living room sitting at Jesus' feet and listening to his words. The Scriptures tell us that Martha was distracted with much serving and went to Jesus and said, "Lord, do you not care that my sister has left me to serve alone? Tell her then to help me" (Luke 10:40). In this instance Mary was criticized by her sister for not helping in the kitchen.

The third instance in which we see Mary at Jesus' feet occurred at another dinner in their home after Lazarus had been raised from the dead. Martha served as usual, but without complaint, and Lazarus sat at the table with Jesus. Mary was moved by her love for the Lord to express her gratitude to him for all that he had meant and all that he had done for each of them. She brought forth a container of expensive ointment and anointed, not his head, but his feet and wiped them with her hair.

The Scriptures tell us that the whole house was filled with the sweet smell of Mary's gift. In a house there are all kinds of odors. There are odors that drift in from the outside. Where there has been a lot of cooking, the smell of food fills the air. When a number of people are gathered, various body scents can be noticed. However, after Mary finished anointing the feet of Jesus, only the sweet smell of her offering was evident. The aftermath from her act of love was more powerful than anything else.

When love fills a home, it is able to absorb much. Poverty can be absorbed and overcome if love is present. People can be happy with little if love is present. And if love is not present, then no matter how much people have, they will still be miserable. When love is present, people will work together to lift themselves out of poverty; but when love isn't present, they will continue to work apart. When love is present, we are able to absorb and forgive the imperfections we see in others. When love is present, we are able to see a person's good qualities in spite of the bad. But when love leaves, all we're able to see is what a person lacks. When love is present in a church, misunderstandings, petty grudges, bitterness, and hostile attitudes are absorbed. Instead of division and confusion, coldness and indifference, when love is present in the church, we're able to say:

There's a sweet, sweet Spirit in this place,
And I know that it's the Spirit of the Lord;

There are sweet expressions on each face,
And I know they feel the presence of the Lord.

Sweet Holy Spirit, Sweet heavenly Dove,
Stay right here with us, Filling us with your love;
And for these blessings we lift our hearts in praise;
Without a doubt we'll know that we have been revived
When we shall leave this place.[1]

Without Thanksgiving, all we would notice would be our problems. But Thanksgiving comes, and we turn our attention away from the distracting scents of trouble and are enraptured by the sweet smell of God's love and goodness toward us, in spite of all. Without Christmas, all we might notice would be the strange odors of war and violence. But Christmas comes with its scent of love to declare peace on earth and goodwill toward people. Without Calvary, without Good Friday, all we would notice would be the strange smell of sin, but Calvary's message about love's sacrifice leaves the lasting scent of redemption. Without Easter, all we would notice would be death's reign over us, but Easter comes with its message of love's triumph, and death loses its sting and the grave its victory.

One thing love cannot absorb, however, is the rigidity of a cold heart that refuses to be absorbed by it. There are none so blind as those who refuse to see. There are none so ignorant as those who refuse to learn. There are none so stubborn as those who refuse to be led. There are no hearts so stony as those who refuse to be touched by love. While some were refreshed by Mary's act, Judas and a few others were offended by it. There will always be those who are offended by the generosity of love. There will always be those who will look upon the openhandedness and generosity of love as a waste. Fortunately, most of us were not around when God created the world. Some of us would have counseled God to give us a plain earth to live on, without any of the beauty that God's love poured into it. Some humans would have advised God, "Make a simple valley floor. Why spend your energy on flowers to brighten it? Why don't you simply make birds to fly; why spend divine

---

[1]"Sweet, Sweet Spirit," by Doris Akers. Copyright 1962—Renewed 1990 by MANNA MUSIC, INC., 25510 Ave. Stanford, Valencia, CA 91355. International Copyright Secured. All Rights Reserved. Used by Permission.

energy on bestowing them with beautiful colors to fascinate the eye and songs to titillate the ear? Just make plain fish; why spend divine energy creating so many varieties of sea life that we humans will never even be able to discover and catalog them all? Just create human beings with only a need for basic communication; why spend divine energy creating humans that express themselves in writing poetry and literature? Just make one or two colors; why spend so much divine energy on all possible variations that humans will waste time on art?"

Certainly if we had been in heaven to behold human sin, we would have seen God's coming to us as a Babe born in mean circumstances. We would have seen Jesus turn down the kingdoms of this world so that he could accept a cross. We would have looked at a blackened sky, a reeling earth, a crown of thorns, and a bleeding Savior and asked God why divine love was spent on the redemption of such human beings.

When Mary expressed her love, she was criticized by those whom one might least expect. Once she was criticized by her own sister, and the other time she was criticized by one of the Lord's disciples. Unjustified or unfair criticism can be disheartening when it comes from places where we least expect it—from family and friends close to our heart or from those who are supposed to be close to Jesus. We can understand criticism coming from the outside world, from the scribes and Pharisees, but not from Jesus' disciples, Jesus' preachers, Jesus' officers, Jesus' church members—those whom we expect to believe and stand for certain things. Even then we must not be too harsh on those who don't understand our love. After all, they haven't sat where we have sat. They were back in the kitchen or at the other end of the table; thus, they don't know what he said to us. They don't understand the relationship between the two of us. We cannot allow their lack of comprehension or their criticism to stop us from expressing the love that we feel.

Mary was criticized because in both instances in which she expressed admiration and love she broke with custom and tradition. When Mary sat at Jesus' feet, she was in the posture of a student. David sat before the Lord as a student and listened for God's voice. Paul wrote about being brought up at the "feet of Gamaliel." In that culture a rabbi taught by positioning himself in a high chair, and his students sat on the ground so that they were literally at their

master's feet. The student's role, however, was usually reserved for men. Women were expected to be where Martha
was, in the kitchen, not at the feet of the Master teacher,
learning about the deep things of life. When Mary anointed
the Lord with ointment, she unbound her hair and wiped
his feet. In that era no self-respecting woman would appear
in public with her hair unbound. On the day a girl was married, her hair was bound and she would never be seen in
public again with her long tresses flowing. Unbound hair
was a sign of a loose woman.

When we have sat at Jesus' feet and his love has filled
our lives, we feel free—free to dream, free to think new
thoughts, free to love, free to try the unusual, free to get out
of the place that society has prescribed for us. For that person whom the Son set free is free indeed. When we have
been freed by Jesus' liberating love, we can express ourselves in ways that we once felt we could not. We feel free to
let tears of joy flow. We feel free enough to clap and wave our
hands in praise to God. We feel free enough to shout "Halle-
lujah" and testify about the goodness of the Lord. We feel
free enough to walk down the aisle to stretch out on God's
word and join the church.

If others pass the wrong judgment and misunder-
stand our actions, that's all right. Others may question why
we're joining the church at this point in our lives. The world
may say we're crazy to give like we give, go like we go, and
do what we do. The world may say we're just emotional, de-
pressed, under stress, drunk, or unlearned. However, if we
are sincere and our spirit is right, we believe that the right
one will get the right message. Jesus, the lover of our souls,
will understand.

Mary was right in believing that Jesus would understand, because both times when her love was criticized, he
came to her rescue. She didn't have to say a word; he defended her and fought her battles. He told her sister,
"Martha, Martha, you are distracted and anxious about
many things, not all of which are related to the kingdom.
One thing is needful, that you center yourself in my word so
that you can be saved. Mary has chosen the good portion,
which shall not be taken away from her." He told Judas,
"Leave her alone. This is her ointment purchased with her
money, earned by her labor. You haven't contributed anything to it, so you have nothing to say about it. Leave her
alone and let her express herself as God's Spirit has directed

her. Leave her alone; what she is doing is in preparation for my burial. The poor you always have with you. Any time you desire, you can do something for the poor. Her kindness does not stop you from doing something for the poor. Let her express her love to me while she can, because she will only have me a little while."

When love is criticized, don't worry about it.

If when you give the best of your service,
Telling the world that the Savior is come;
Be not dismayed when men don't believe you;
He understands; He'll say, "Well done."

Oh, when I come to the end of my journey,
Weary of life and the battle is won;
Carrying the staff and cross of redemption,
He'll understand, and say "Well done."[2]

2From "He Understands, He'll Say 'Well Done,' " by Lucie E. Campbell.

13

Mary Magdalene:
A Love That Won't Let Go

Matthew 27:57–61
Suzan D. Johnson Cook

When it was evening, there came a rich man from Arimathea, named Joseph, who also was a disciple of Jesus. He went to Pilate and asked for the body of Jesus. Then Pilate ordered it to be given to him. And Joseph took the body, and wrapped it in a clean linen shroud, and laid it in his own new tomb, which he had hewn in the rock; and he rolled a great stone to the door of the tomb, and departed. Mary Magdalene and the other Mary were there, sitting opposite the sepulchre (Matthew 27:57–61).

It had been a long road with many winding turns. From the first day that Mary Magdalene had heard about Jesus, there was something special that had happened to and for her. She was no longer the same woman. Not only had she had a spiritual encounter, but also she had learned that a person is a union of mind, body, and spirit, and that for her to be all that she needed to be, she needed to be made whole. And Jesus of Galilee had done this for her, a woman of Magdala. Seven demons had been cast out of her; a wonderful change in her life had been wrought, and she became one of the most devoted disciples.

She had been with Jesus when he traveled throughout Galilee, ministering in villages and cities where they would listen and learn. Had he not declared that his yoke could be taken and that they could learn of him? Several other women accompanied her, and they had become quite close. Among them were Joanna, the wife of Chuza, Herod's steward; and Susanna. Certainly Mary Magdalene had also become close with Mary, Jesus' mother. Many strong relationships developed among these women. Throughout the Word given to us, God seems to be always calling people to right relationships with God and with one another. From the onset of creation, relationships—both intimate ones and those involving considerable distance—were central to our seeing how some powerful things could happen for those who were willing to connect and stick with the situation in spite of prevailing circumstances.

The Old Testament reminds us of Ruth, the Moabite woman, who was drawn to her mother-in-law in the midst of famine, idolatry, and grief. Yet she persevered, saying to her mother-in-law, Naomi, "Entreat me not to leave you . . . ; your people shall be my people, and your God my God. . . ." Then there was Queen Esther, who married into royalty, who with all of her status and even her life on the line, stood on a principle and pleaded for her people, God's people, so that salvation would come for an entire race, declaring, "If I perish, I perish."

First Kings draws us intimately into the relationship between a woman who is referred to as the widow of Zarephath and the prophet Elijah. Both of them were forced to meet each other's needs at a time when both were undergoing spiritual surgery and were being tested concerning their call and trust relationship with God. Still, they came together in the midst of death, suffering, and pain, when the woman and her son were down to their last cruse of oil, and after Elijah had been fed by ravens and chased out of his homeland.

The New Testament also draws us into various relationships between Jesus and his followers. Often we recall the encounter between Jesus and the two sisters, Mary and Martha, after their brother, Lazarus, died. It was, I believe, more than just a story about death; it also is a story that allows us to see the depth of the relationship between Jesus and Lazarus and Jesus' humanness as well. Over and over again, whether we are invited to witness Jesus calling someone into a lifetime of ministry or whether it is just an encounter that leads someone to choose a committed life, we find that the family of God is more than just a theme—it is a reality.

Today's text in Matthew 27 compels us once again to look at a scenario when Jesus was connected with others.

However, this time Jesus is the recipient of the love rather than the one who gave the love. It is indeed a story of the Word being made flesh amongst us. This story takes place just after one of the most powerful events in human history, the cross at Calvary. This one event would change the course of history for Christians forevermore. It was the blending of the old and the new, and the ushering in of a new era—the advent of respecting and connecting with that which God had been in the beginning.

Mary was there, alongside so many others. They had been afraid to speak out, and even if they could have spoken, what would they have said? Somehow, even though they had heard all of Jesus' teachings and had sat at his feet with the multitudes, his words had not hit home until the moment of his crucifixion. Just one week ago a crowd had cheered as Jesus rode into Jerusalem. Even though he had spoken about his death, when there is a close relationship, people sometimes feel they can change things that are already on their course and meant to be.

As Mary Magdalene stood at the cross, the emblem of suffering and shame, perhaps she thought back to her moment of ministry with him. Maybe she wondered what was going through the mind of Jesus' mother as she saw the pain and agony etched in her friend's face. She had listened closely when Jesus told Mary to go with John. She knew that they would form a new family structure, a new mother/son relationship. But even though it would make sense logically, emotionally there were still attachments that were not so easy to rearrange. Mary Magdalene wanted to reach out and let Jesus' mother know that she was praying for and with her, but right at that time she found it hard to pray for herself. It was not as easy to let go as she had thought. The time of departure was at hand, but she was not ready for Jesus to depart from her. It was difficult. Finally, after the grueling moments that she witnessed, after having seen so many soldiers lose their dignity and respect as they began playing with her Lord as though he were nothing, she probably understood that these moments were the true test of her faith. There comes a time in every relationship when one must look at oneself introspectively, and even retrospectively, and sort out the real from the imagined and learn to live with what is happening at that moment.

She looked around and saw that the soldiers were all gone; most of the onlookers had also left the scene. The last will and testament for Jesus' mother was in order; salvation had been granted for a thief on a cross; human body functions and nurturing needs had been dealt with as Jesus uttered some of his final words, saying, "I thirst," and "My God, My God, why hast thou forsaken me? (Eli, Eli, lama sabachthani?)" And even though the people who had been observing were now silent, it was their fears and their tears which were now speaking. All of those whom she had come to know as believers and followers had a soul connection. There was still something between them that a cross could not manage to snuff out, something that became even more strongly renewed as the blood was forced out. Maybe it had something to do with Jesus' commending his spirit into the hands of God as he uttered his last breath. He could not have left her just like that. He had promised that he would come again.

After the agony, the suffering, and the shame, she overheard the conversation between Joseph and the graveyard manager. Joseph, a rich man from a place called Arimathea, at first had difficulty receiving the Word, but after a while, he converted and gave his life to Jesus and was a follower. Now he, too, wanted to have some connection with Jesus, and so he offered his tomb for the Lord to insure that the same respect and dignity that he had had while he lived would not be removed from him in his death. So, he voluntarily offered his own personal gravesite for this One who had healed and ministered to both himself and so many others throughout Galilee. He was the wounded healer.

Many knew and loved Jesus and had him as part of their lives, but on this day many had gone into hiding, some in their own homes, but others at hideaway places because they feared that they would be caught. The One they had professed to love was now dead; a cross snuffed out their hopes and caused fears to arise. From a cross to a corpse. Trust had trickled out and been replaced by trembling as those in authority and neighbors ridiculed the believers. Even a proper burial for this Jewish man had not been done because, as Jewish law dictated, everything had to be done before sundown on the sabbath. Therefore, the ointments and spices used in other burial ceremonies to preserve and clean the corpse were still in their containers. Now the importance of Mary of Bethany's sharing of her precious ointment with the Lord was coming to light. Her act had been prophetic. It was the Jewish sabbath, and no other opportunity would be afforded to properly prepare the body. But God, being providential and omniscient, took care of all of this ahead of time. Mary of Bethany's alabaster vessel now had more significance than ever before. Many had gone, but two refused to go. No more soldiers present, no disciples; only two women remained—two refused to let go. Love is patient and love is kind, and love is greater than even hope.

As Joseph of Arimathea departed, two women sat opposite the tomb. One was simply referred to as "the other Mary," but Mary Magdalene, this woman of God, is clearly named. Too much had transpired between Mary Magdalene and Jesus for her not to believe that the One who led her beside still waters and restored her soul would also be with her in these moments of stillness. Usually a tomb represented death, but now it was just the beginning of a new lease on life. Perhaps to pass the time she was reciting David's forty-sixth psalm: "Be still and know that I am God." She was determined. She was dedicated. She had a love that refused to let go, a love that would remain forever, for better, for worse, and not even affected by death.

The heavenly record was now revealing itself. Mary Magdalene loved Jesus. Mary Magdalene believed enough not only to look at surface appearances but also to use her spiritual vision to see beneath and beyond the tomb. That spiritual vision would lead her into her own heart and connect her with a God who would be bold enough and miraculous enough to roll the sealed stone away. Jesus had preached and talked about sacrifice. Now he had done it for her, and she was willing to sacrifice whatever it took, especially her time, to do something for him.

At sunrise there was a surprise. Not only was the grave opened and the stone rolled away, but the Lord's body was not there. He had risen, just like he had said he would, for he loved us too much to renege and let go. He recalled his own promise, which had to be fulfilled, that on the third day he would rise again, and that a Comforter would come. Later, at his homegoing celebration, Jesus gave this promise: "Lo, I am with you always, to the close of the age."

Which women are willing to wait on the Lord and to be of good courage, with enough love to sustain, despite the moments of uncertainty and even rejection by others who have not learned how to love? This is the challenge of the church, especially as it ministers to singles, teaching those who may have been cast out by others in relationships that had previously embodied love, to discern and identify those relationships that are really loving. Love means sacrifice; love means waiting, even when you are not sure. But, most importantly, love is reciprocal. It always gives back. Jesus loved Mary Magdalene. Mary Magdalene loved Jesus. By her efforts she was the new forerunner, not like John the Baptist, who had said, "Behold, the lamb of God who takes away the sins of the world," but a trail blazer for all women who will dare to carry God's word. She could now announce to those who were not present at the tomb that Jesus was alive and that he wanted them to go to Jerusalem, where they were to wait for power and a Comforter. In Jesus' resurrection we are all connected to and with God, as long as we understand that even today the stones are rolled away and that God's love won't let us go.

14

Mary Magdalene:
When Love Lingers

Matthew 27:57–61

William D. Watley

"You might as well leave now. There's nothing else to be done for the present. It's over." These may have been the words of Joseph of Arimathea to Mary Magdalene as the great stone was rolled in place at the door of the tomb, which completed the hastily arranged burial of Jesus. Mary had been sitting quietly in a state of stunned grief, observing as Joseph completed the burial transactions for Jesus. *He is actually dead; they have killed my Lord,* Mary thought to herself. Her eyes were red and puffy from tears of sorrow that had silently run down her cheeks and dropped to the ground, even as her Lord's sweat had as he bore the cross, and even as his blood had when he was pierced in the side. *Will the tears ever stop flowing?* she asked herself. A couple of times she thought she was "cried out" and that her tear ducts were dry. However, every time she thought about the events of the last twenty-four hours, every time she thought about the fact that Jesus, whom she loved as much as she loved her own life, was dead and gone forever, the tears would start flowing again.

Mary Magdalene was one of those who had been loving and courageous enough to have stood by our Lord to the very end. She was present at our Lord's crucifixion and burial because following Jesus had become the pattern for her life. Some only followed him on special occasions— when he was passing through their towns. Others followed him when they wanted something from him. But Mary Magdalene was part of that small group of women who, along with the disciples, had followed him from place to place. In time she had become one of his strongest and most visible supporters.

91

Mary Magdalene is mentioned fourteen times in the Gospels. Eight of those times when she is mentioned with other women, her name leads the list. She is mentioned alone five times in passages relating to the death and resurrection of Jesus. In one instance her name comes after those of the mother and aunt of Jesus. Along with them and others she had stood by the cross of Jesus, but because of their relation to the Master, they were mentioned first. It would not have been proper to list Mary Magdalene's name before Jesus' relatives. If Simon Peter and John, the beloved, were foremost among the male disciples, then Mary was foremost among the women followers, and probably she was our Lord's closest female friend.

The Scriptures do not tell us when Jesus and Mary met. The Gospels of Mark and Luke state that Jesus had cured Mary of seven demons. Some have interpreted the reference to seven demons to mean that Mary Magdalene was a wicked woman, or a prostitute, before she met Jesus. A custom later arose of naming agencies or shelters that ministered to fallen women and wayward girls as "Magdalene homes." The Scriptures, however, do not give any basis for such a harsh assessment of her character. In the Gospels, Mary Magdalene is always held in high regard.

In the time that the New Testament was written, all sickness, whether physical or mental, was regarded as evil or the work of the devil. If someone was born with a birth defect, it was believed that he or she had reaped evil because of somebody's sin. If someone became ill, it was believed that he or she had been assaulted by evil or possessed by demons. Most current New Testament scholars believe that Mary's condition was mental, not moral. If this is true, she probably suffered from periods of insanity. Whether Mary's condition came through heredity or some crisis in her life, we do not know.

The number seven in Scripture represents wholeness or completeness. Thus, when the Bible says that Mary Magdalene was possessed by seven demons, it may mean that there were times when she was totally dominated by the evil affliction that came upon her and that caused her to suffer much. Mary, then, would have been a tormented person with no hope of a normal life, before she met Jesus. Like the demon-possessed man known as Legion, Mary Magdalene was troubled by many things. Her behavior may not have been as wild and erratic as Legion's, but her mind was disoriented, her spirit confused, and her appearance disheveled. When one's mind and spirit are not at peace, one's appearance is also affected.

At some point the lives of Jesus and Mary from Magdala crossed, and he did for her what he had done for so many others. He healed her; he touched her, and, oh, the joy that flooded her soul. He brought peace to her mind and spirit, and she became a new creation. Gone were the alternating wild and hollow looks; gone were the sunken cheeks and unkempt hair; gone were the voices in her head that drove her to do strange things; gone were the bizarre thoughts that disrupted her life. Mary became a devoted and committed follower of Christ.

Mary is called Magdalene because she came from the village of Magdala, which was located on the coast of Galilee about three miles from Capernaum. Some believe that Mary had been connected with the primitive dye works or textile industry of that community, which would have afforded her the financial resources to support the work of our Lord. Evidently she was single because she was free to follow the Lord. Healed, Mary supported Jesus in his travels so that he might do for others what he had done for her. Healed, Mary devoted herself to the person who had given her life back to her. Mary epitomizes the best of a grateful heart.

We often say that we are grateful to others for what they have done for us. How do we show our gratitude? By our willingness to give back and invest in those who have done so much for us. A thankful heart and a grudging spirit are contradictions. Mouths that are open with praise and hands that are closed to giving are inconsistent actions. If one is truly thankful, then one cannot be cheap and stingy at the same time. Selfishness asks, "What can I get?" Ingratitude asks, "What can I keep?" Thanksgiving asks, "What can I give?" It was a thankful heart that prompted David to ask:

> *What shall I render to the Lord*
> *for all his bounty to me?*
> *I will lift up the cup of salvation*
> *and call on the name of the Lord,*
> *I will pay my vows to the Lord*
> *in the presence of all his people . . .*
> *—Psalm 116:12 – 13*

Mary Magdalene's thankful heart was realistic. She understood that Jesus and the disciples needed money, like everybody else, and had little. One of the most amazing facts of history is that a poor man stands at its center. The individual whose life has done the most to redeem the history and transform the future of humanity was not the ruler of a great empire like Genghis Khan or Charlemagne. Nor was he a great general like Alexander the Great or Napoleon; nor was he a financier like Andrew Carnegie or John Rockefeller. Neither was he a scientist like Isaac Newton or Albert Einstein. History stands or falls on the life of a poor man. The purest and most noble life in the history of all humanity was that of a poor man. The name that devils fear and before which angels and humans fall to confess as Lord, belonged to a man who was so poor that when he died, all he owned was the robe he wore on his back.

Jesus was so poor that he had to depend upon the goodness of others to eat. He could have turned the stones in the road into bread and the water he drank into wine. But he never used his powers or gifts for himself—only and always for others. Thus, he had nothing, yet he had everything because he had people who loved him enough to provide whatever he needed. Nobody who has the loyalty, love, and respect of others will ever be poor. Nobody who has loving friends to help provide for them is poor. Jesus and Mary Magdalene made a good team. She helped provide the physical and financial support that he needed; he gave her the spiritual nourishment that her life needed. They each gave to the other. Those are always the best relationships—those that are generous enough to give to each other and mature enough to receive from each other. In some relationships one party always gives while the other always receives. Sometimes the one who is receiving believes he or she has nothing to give, and thus offers nothing. Sometimes the giver is too proud to receive anything from the other. But Mary Magdalene and Jesus gave to each other.

Now let us note that it took courage for Mary to support Jesus. Can we imagine how it must have looked to the sick, petty, and trashy minds of that era for a single woman such as Mary Magdalene to follow a single man such as Jesus around the countryside? Can't we just imagine the cruel things that people may have said about Jesus and Mary? Some undoubtedly said that Jesus was taking advantage of her, that he had cast some sort of spell over her, that he was taking her for a ride, and that he was after all he could get. Some probably talked about how she was running after Jesus in the hopes of fulfilling her fantasies. Imagine some of the good sisters at Jacob's well or the brothers gathered in the marketplace as they said, "Ain't it a shame how she's running after him? Everywhere you see him, you see her. Where there's smoke, there's fire. Something's got to be going on."

Mary Magdalene, however, knew what she was about, and so did Jesus. If we know what we're about, if Jesus knows what we're about (and he does), if we are being blessed and receiving joy from our service, then we have no reason to be ashamed or to fear idle talk. I believe that when Mary was healed, she decided to follow Jesus and help him whenever and however she could. He would not personally accept any of her money, so she would help in whatever ways she could for as long as she could.

Thus, she followed him to the end. She followed him through his ups and downs. She was with him when the crowds sang his praise, and she was with him when they turned against him. She heard the Palm Sunday crowd shout, "Hosanna!" and she heard the Thursday night mob yell, "Crucify him!" She wept when she saw her magnificent Savior after he had been scourged by Pilate—bloodied and bound, a crown of thorns on his head, and a reed scepter in his hands. She saw Pontius Pilate point to her Lord and say, "Behold your King." She saw her Lord led away with two criminals, carrying the beam of the cross upon his shoulders. She saw him every time he stumbled and fell. She saw the Roman soldiers place the cross upon the shoulders of Simon, the black African. She saw Simon do what she had been doing and what she wanted to do then—follow in the footsteps of Jesus. She and others were there when Jesus turned to them and said: "Daughters of Jerusalem, do not weep for me, but weep for yourselves and your children."

She saw Jesus nailed to the cross. She saw him, as the old preachers used to say, when they hung him high and stretched him wide. It took courage for Mary to linger near the cross. Mary's love in the hour of Jesus' death showed the same commitment as it had shown during his life. As her love had not feared the criticism and reproach of those who did not understand her actions as she supported Jesus' ministry, so her love did not fear the reproach of the Roman soldiers as she lingered near the cross.

Mary was there when the body of Jesus was taken down from the cross, and she was there when it was laid in Joseph's tomb. When the stone was rolled to the door, Mary Magdalene was still there. As she started toward her dwelling, I imagine that she thought to herself, *Whoever would have thought that it would end like this? Whoever would have thought that a life so noble, so full of love and goodness, would come to such a tragic end? Whoever would have thought that a life with so much to offer would end up on a cross at such an early age.* However, Mary had this consolation: She had kept her vow and followed Jesus to the end. No matter how badly things had turned out, she had done what she was supposed to do.

Sometimes things don't turn out as we would like them, but if our love has been faithful, we can receive consolation in knowing that we have done what we were supposed to do. Sometimes our marriages don't work out. We can give our all, but it still takes three to make a marriage work—the husband, the wife, and God. If our spouse doesn't do his or her part, and we know that we have done our best, we have the consolation of knowing that we have done what we were supposed to do; all we can do is what we're supposed to do.

Sometimes our children don't turn out as we might desire. The streets can turn the heads of young people from their home training. But if, as parents, we have tried to raise them in the church and provide the best home we can and live the right kind of life before them, at some point they must make their decision about whom they will serve and the kind of men and women they will be. Sometimes their choices hurt us, but if we've done what we're supposed to do, all we can do is leave them in the hands of the Lord and linger on our knees and pray that they will come to themselves before it is eternally too late.

Sometimes situations don't turn out as we desire. In spite of our prayers, loved ones don't get well. The programs we sponsor from a sincere heart fall below our expectations. But if we have given our all, we can still hold our heads up because we have done what we're supposed to do. Sometimes after I preach nobody joins the church, and I can't see that any hardened attitudes have been changed.

I'm not sure that my message has really been heard or done any good. But at least I have this consolation—that I have fulfilled my vow; I've done what I'm supposed to do.

As Mary Magdalene left the tomb, I imagine that she vowed to return. According to John's Gospel, on the first day of the week Mary came to the tomb while it was still dark and saw the stone rolled away and ran to tell Peter and John. They ran back to the tomb and left, but Mary kept lingering. Because she kept lingering, she heard a voice they didn't hear. Jesus called her by her name. Because she kept lingering, she saw what they didn't see. She saw Jesus Christ, her resurrected Lord. Because she lingered, she has the distinction of being the first person to see Jesus in the glory of his resurrection.

Lingering love may seem like wasted love and energy. But the lesson of Mary Magdalene's example is that lingering love is rewarded. If we stay when others leave, keep going when others stop, draw near when others draw away, are faithful when others desert, live right when others compromise, stay on our knees when others give up, keep loving when others lose patience, believe when others doubt, give freely when others scrimp, give our all when others hold back, we shall see Jesus in his glory. Our lingering love will be rewarded. Across the ages his promise comes to those who are possessed with a lingering love: "Be faithful unto death, and I will give you the crown of life" (Revelation 2:10).

15

Mary, the Mother of Jesus:
Blessed Among Women

Luke 1:26–31 (KJV)
Suzan D. Johnson Cook

And in the sixth month the angel Gabriel was sent from God unto a city of Galilee, named Nazareth, to a virgin espoused to a man whose name was Joseph, of the house of David; and the virgin's name was Mary. And the angel came in unto her, and said, Hail, thou that art highly favoured, the Lord is with thee: blessed art thou among women. And when she saw him, she was troubled at his saying, and cast in her mind what manner of salutation this should be. And the angel said unto her, Fear not, Mary: for thou hast found favour with God. And, behold, thou shalt conceive in thy womb, and bring forth a son, and shalt call his name JESUS (Luke 1:26 – 31, KJV).

There are times in this Christian walk when no one but you really knows what the Lord is doing with you. There are times when others just do not understand because there is no logical or rational reason for your doing what you are doing or being where you are in your personal and professional life, but within your heart and spirit, you know and God knows. Sometimes that is really all you have to stand on. Such was the case with my call to the ordained ministry. Prior to my acceptance of my call, I was in a popular profession, with much visibility and a lucrative financial situation. I was a television producer with all of the major networks at a time when the racial climate was such that there was a demand for black women such as myself to be in the industry. In fact, I could write "my own ticket" pretty much anywhere in the country. Yet after the very long hours that I had to put in, after finishing the day's challenges and leaving the sets, after meeting the leading political figures and entertainment stars in the country—I was not fulfilled. There was still an insatiable desire to serve the Lord in a full-time capacity.

I first thought that if I could take a few seminary courses here and there, perhaps this feeling would go away. Many people thought it was just a religious fervor and zeal that would soon pass away. I enrolled in courses up and down the east coast as my various television assignments would carry me to various cities. I remember well the last stop in my television career. I was in Miami, and I knew that it was time to do what I felt called to do. After resigning my job as a producer, I went to New York, enrolled full-time in seminary, and took a position working full-time in the communications field. But even then, there came a time when I had to choose whom I would serve. As the Ecclesiastical writer said, "To everything there is a season, and a time to every purpose under the heaven" (Ecclesiastes 3:1, KJV). Putting down the secular security, I picked up my faith and chose to go into full-time ministry without anything more than the promise that God would provide.

To my family, peers, and colleagues, who were Christians, but not called, my decision seemed to be the craziest move I had ever made. It was not consistent with the career path they expected me to pursue. But I knew that God had called me. There are these times in the Christian walk when no one understands but you and God. But no one else really needs to understand your walk, for it is your walk, and in time God will reveal and confirm that which was yours to do.

Mary, Jesus' mother, was a young teen-age woman who experienced a series of circumstances that most people were not spiritually prepared to comprehend. Certainly in this village there were expected roles for women, particularly those who were engaged to be married. Plans for the wedding day were, no doubt, being made, but God had other plans. God had sought her out to be the vessel through whom the prophetic promises would be fulfilled. Mary's child was to be the one who would come to save the people from their sins. His name had already been selected; the mission was already in place; a forerunner, John, was divinely predestined; God's agenda was clear. Jesus would come into the world. Jesus would be born to a virgin woman by immaculate conception. And the angels would declare that this ordinary woman named Mary was "blessed among women" and the instrument through whom God worked.

To her neighbors and to those in authority, Mary would not have been selected for anything so major in history. But God elevates those persons we consider insignificant in order to demonstrate that the power of the gospel can penetrate class, social, racial, and ethnic lines. God can work despite the limitations of humanity. The gospel, the Word in flesh, would be a liberator to set the captives free—a power for the Jews and also for the Gentiles.

Mary was engaged to Joseph, a carpenter. Perhaps wedding plans had been established, but certainly not a premarital pregnancy. Logically it made no sense, but spiritually it made all the sense in the world.

The Holy Spirit came to Mary to impregnate her with the Christ child. The heavens rejoiced, but on earth Mary became the victim of emotional abuse and societal pressures. She was forced in her ninth month of pregnancy to deal with an old tax law, which was resurrected from the archives, that would mean she would have to travel when she was at greatest risk. And to top all of the foreseen dangers, there was the unforeseen rejection of Mary and Joseph when they learned that for various reasons, there was "no room in the inn." What a feeling she must have had, knowing that God had interrupted her life and chosen her to do a task, yet having all the doors closed at the time she was ready to deliver.

How many women feel as Mary did—trapped in what seemingly are no-win situations, yet strong in their faith that God is really with them? Often when women receive invitations to participate in God's work, they are not really welcome. I recall an incident in my first year of pastoring. I, along with my church, was invited to help a local congregation celebrate its annual Women's Day. Because of my visibility at the time, the pastor felt a large crowd would gather because of name recognition. Once we arrived and the crowd had gathered, however, it was quite evident that that was all they wanted from us. After my sermon, and after two souls had given their lives to the Lord, the pastor proceeded to tear my sermon apart and talk about the need to slow down the movement of women into the ministry. Well, my congregation was ready to walk out, but I had to understand that my witness was still important because God used me in spite of the pastor's own selfish desires. We remained through the end of the service, yet the reality set in—there still was "no room in the inn."

Perhaps that is why Scripture tells us that Mary pondered some things in her heart, because it is not always wise to move immediately and hastily, even though one may be armed with knowledge. God's timing may not call for immediate action. Mary knew that it was the Christ inside of her, and those designated by God also knew: Joseph, her espoused; wise men from the East; shepherds abiding in their fields by night; cousin Elizabeth; and Anna and Simeon. God had a time for the good news to be revealed. God's agenda cannot be vetoed.

Despite the gifts that were brought to her and the Christ child, in spite of the blessings in the temple, Mary also had to deal with mothering one who was not an ordinary child. He was a child who would grow in wisdom, stature, and grace, and one whose death date had already been determined. She had to deal with his questioning the rabbis in the temple and watch as he stood before the crowds in the synagogue and read to them from the book of the prophet Isaiah: "The Spirit of the Lord is upon me. . . ." Mary had to understand that he would not be the normal carpentry apprentice, but that soon he would be about "his Father's business." Nor would he become a Galilean fisherman, but instead would teach those Galileans how to become "fishers of men." There was some wrestling, I am sure, with just how much to trust God and how to deal with the very real humanity that young adult women face when handling their own fears about themselves and their children.

Often I see young mothers, some with husbands, but most often as single parents, who are wrestling with their sexuality and their need for companionship, while at the same time trying to understand what God is doing with them, not just as parents, but in terms of a calling on their lives. They want to carry Christ with them, yet pressures mount, and they do not always have the support systems around them that will understand. These parents, too, must stand on the blessed assurance that Jesus is with them. And in giving birth to Christ in their new lives, these young "Marys," despite the odds, can compose and sing in their spirit their modern-day versions of the Magnificat, as their souls magnify the Lord.

Mary could sing because God's anointing and confirmation came to her, showing her a foretaste of divine glory. For later, that same son whom she saw and heard preaching to thousands; healing persons suffering from lameness and blindness; casting demons out of her friends; settling disputes amongst leaders—that same son would be unjustly and mercilessly tried as she sat praying for him. She would witness a terribly painful crucifixion, and even have her own life and care placed into the responsibility of John. What do you imagine her song was like then?

But praise be to God. On a Sunday, a third day, Mary heard that the grave was empty, that the seal of the tomb had been broken. And all of the messages that had come to her, from that first day of conception until this day of resurrection, became clear. This was all part of God's plan. God could not be outdone. In being a willing participant in God's will for the world, Mary could receive her salvation and now be a witness unto the uttermost parts of the world.

Motherhood, wifehood, and servanthood were now inextricably juxtaposed to help her to be a delivered disciple. She was not a son of thunder, but she became a woman of wonder, from obscurity in a remote village to a place in God's history book, to be revealed to the whole world. Mary, indeed, showed us that the "blest of us will help the rest of us."

16

Mary, the Mother of Jesus:
Bringing Forth God's Best

Luke 2:7a
William D. Watley

About fourteen years ago I heard a minister announce a sermon subject that I have never forgotten. This in itself is no small feat. As a regular worshiper and active participant in church, I have heard a number of sermons across the years, most of which I have forgotten. On the next day or even the next hour after hearing a sermon, if you had asked what the preacher spoke about, I would have had to ponder as I tried to remember. With some sermons that I have heard during my years of church attendance, if I had been asked what the preacher was talking about while he was in the midst of his delivery, or even as he spoke, I wouldn't have been able to tell you. As a preacher, I have delivered hundreds of sermons, many of which are eminently forgettable, even to me. Yet, during all of my hearing and delivering and remembering and forgetting over the years, the title of this particular sermon has remained with me. The title of the preacher's message to which I have been referring was "God Don't Sponsor No Flops."

Admittedly the sermon title leaves much to be desired in terms of its grammar and syntax. A couple of years ago while in a worship service, I was sitting next to a preacher who had spent a number of years teaching in the public school system. We were listening as another preacher murdered the English language as he spoke. After observing him, the preacher next to me whispered, "If I could just get him in a classroom for one month, I could really do something with him." When the grammar and construction of this sermon title are examined, a number of English teachers could rightly feel the same way or wish the same thing. Yet despite the faulty grammar of this title, the thought behind it is profound, and its message ought never be forgotten—"God Don't Sponsor No Flops." In other words, God does not make failures or create mediocrity. God creates people to be productive; God creates us to aspire to the highest and the best, and to reach those goals.

When we were created, God put the best in us. God only uses the best of everything. The light bulbs that we use soon burn out. Even the long-lasting bulbs eventually burn out. But the light that God produces in the universe is the best possible light. The stars that we see at night are the same ones that Jacob observed as he lay on his back in the desert stretches of the wilderness and saw angels ascending and descending on a ladder to heaven. They are the same stars that looked down upon the wilderness wanderings of the Hebrews. David looked up at them as he wrote the psalms, and Daniel reflected upon them in Babylon. They served as the background to that peculiarly bright star that guided the wise men to the child Jesus. Columbus used them to find a new world, and Copernicus and Galileo used them to discover the movement of the earth in space. They still twinkle to inspire, and they still shine to brighten an otherwise ominous blackened sky. The light that God used for the stars is truly long-lasting and truly the best.

The heat that God gave the sun to warm the earth is truly the best and most penetrating and enduring heat available. Although the sun is ninety-three million miles away, someone has said that it radiates more energy in one second than humankind has used since the beginning of civilization. Despite its distance from us, its rays are still powerful enough to give us sunstroke in the summer, if we're not careful. Its heat is so powerful that within the stratosphere there is a protective shield, an ozone layer, to dilute the power of some of its rays. Even in the winter when it is farthest from us, the sun is still powerful enough to sustain life on the earth. God used the best and most powerful heat to warm this planet.

I believe that this same God used the best when human beings, the crowning glory of the creation, were made. God, who used the most enduring light for the stars and the most penetrating heat for the sun, would not have scrimped and used shoddy materials for us. Although we were made from the dust of the earth, it was dust that was endowed with eternity. God blew into us the breath of life, and we became living souls. Let us never forget that we are made by the best, from the best, to be the best. We are not made from cheap materials and thrown together carelessly with poor workmanship. Once I was shaking hands with some parishioners at the close of a worship service. I greeted a fine-looking lady in her eighties who was wearing an attractive fur stole. As I greeted her, I admired her fur and said, "Good morning. You're looking mighty nice this morning. You're somebody." She looked at me and said, "I know I am—God made me that way." We were not created to be gutter, low-life people. We were created a little lower than the angels; we were created to be somebody. God has put within us the potential for greatness because "God Don't Sponsor No Flops."

The question that many of us may be asking is, How do we account for the fact that so many of our fellow human beings, made by the same God and endowed with the same potential, are so sorry and lazy? Instead of going from strength to strength and grace to glory, some of us seem to be journeying from grace to disgrace, and from flop to flop, and failure to failure. To avoid the pitfalls of failing and flopping so that we might bring forth the best, let us look at the life of Mary, the mother of Jesus.

Our text tells us that "she [Mary] brought forth her firstborn son. . . ." How was Mary enabled to bring forth Jesus? She worked in partnership with God. She nurtured the life that had been placed within her. The angel came to her and told her that she would conceive and bear a son whose name would be called Jesus. When she inquired how this would be accomplished, since she was a virgin, the angel told her that the Holy Spirit would come upon her and the power of the Most High would overshadow her. Thus, her child would be called holy, the Son of God. What Mary brought forth was what God's Spirit had planted within her.

We can only bring forth what the Spirit has planted, and if the Spirit has not planted it, we have no business trying to bring it forth. That's why so many of us are frustrated in our service. We are trying to bring forth that which has not been planted within us. We observe the talents and abilities of others and try to imitate them. At best we become cheap reproductions, and at worst outright failures. We can't bring forth that which is planted within somebody else's life; we can only bring forth that which is planted within our own. We must live within the gifts, limitations, and potential that has been planted within us.

We can get into a lot of trouble by trying to imitate someone else's gifts, potential, and lifestyle. We can make ourselves look like complete idiots by trying to dress, walk, talk, and behave like someone else. I always caution younger ministers about trying to imitate what they see older ministers do. A younger man or woman can quickly get into serious trouble trying to imitate an older, more experienced man or woman—and the opposite is also true. We cannot get away with doing what we see others do; we must live within the limitations and gifts that have been placed within us. Children who observe how other children talk and treat their parents can get into serious trouble by trying to imitate what those children do. Husbands and wives who observe how other folks treat their spouses and try to do the same thing, using the same language and telling the same lies, can get into serious trouble. Anytime we try to be what we're not, we're going to fail, and we can't blame God because "God Don't Sponsor No Flops." We must blame ourselves for rejecting the life within and embracing something that we see without. If we would bring forth the best, we must nurture the gifts and the potential that God has placed within us.

Mary only brought forth that which the Spirit had planted within her. She did not bring forth a Methuselah, who would live long enough to care for her the rest of her days. She did not bring forth a great king like Solomon, who could build her a palace. Although she would be denied some of this life's temporal comforts, she brought forth someone much greater. She brought forth one who would be King of kings, whose reign would know no end. She brought forth God's best, God's only begotten Son. One might be under the impression that to bring forth God's best, Mary must have been some kind of superwoman with specially endowed attributes. According to the Scriptures, however, she was a humble handmaiden. She wasn't a great prophetess like Deborah or a great queen like Esther; she wasn't an astute charmer like Abigail. She was an ordinary handmaiden. The Magnificat emphasizes her ordinariness. After she received the word from the angel, Mary declared: "My soul magnifies the Lord, and my spirit rejoices in God my Savior, for he has regarded the low estate of his handmaiden" (Luke 1:46 – 48).

Sometimes we believe that we must be specially endowed to bring forth God's best. However, when we look at Mary, we discover that God's highest and best was brought forth by an ordinary handmaiden. Great works are often done by ordinary people with extraordinary spirit within. Look at those in our lives, as well as those in history, who have accomplished the most. Many times they are ordinary people with extraordinary spirit, and as they struggled to bring forth that spirit within, greatness has come. When we view the works of Michelangelo, we see the results of his struggle to bring forth that which was within. When we hear the music of Beethoven, Mozart, Aretha Franklin, B.B. King, or Andraé Crouch, we hear the bringing forth of that which was within. When we read the works of Shakespeare or James Weldon Johnson or James Baldwin, we read the results of their struggle to bring forth that which was within. They are all ordinary people who struggled to bring forth that which God had placed within them. Mary was an ordinary handmaiden whose faithfulness to the task of nurturing and struggling to bring forth that which God's Spirit had placed within her made her significant in the history of the world, as the mother of Jesus.

How did Mary bring forth God's son? The Scriptures tell us that when she received the news from the angel, Mary said: "Behold, I am the handmaid of the Lord; let it be to me according to your word" (Luke 1:38). Her aunt, Elizabeth, said of her, "Blessed is she who believed that there would be a fulfillment of what was spoken to her from the Lord" (Luke 1:45). Mary was willing to believe God's word. We bring forth God's best when we are willing to believe God's word. The trouble with most of our faith is that we really don't believe God's word. Some of us are like Sarah, who laughed when she received the word of God that in her old age she would bear a son. Some of us are like Gideon, who asked God to show him a sign when he received the call of God. Some of us are like Jonah, who ran in the opposite direction when he received the word of God. Some of us are like Zechariah, the father of John the Baptist, who questioned and doubted when he received the word of God.

We can't bring forth God's best when we laugh at what seems to be the impossible promise of God's word. We must understand that there is nothing too hard for the Lord. We can't bring forth God's best when we're running from the Lord, for we can't run and we can't hide from the word of the Lord. Like Jonah, we'll discover that whatever we are, wherever we are, wherever we live, irrespective of the circumstances in which we find ourselves, God's word will find us. When I was in Georgia we used to sing, "You can't hide, sinner; you can't hide." We can't bring forth God's best when we're always trying to test or prove the word before we accept it. We walk by faith, not by sight. We cannot bring forth God's best when we are always doubting and questioning the word of God. To bring forth God's best, we must believe God's word as it comes to us. We must be willing to say, as did Mary, "I'm your servant; let it be to me according to your word."

Mary truly believed the word of God. A group of ministers were discussing their problems, their fears, their frustrations, and how the Lord granted them victory in their respective situations. Finally someone arose and said, "The trouble with a number of us is that we don't really believe the gospel we preach. All we have to do is believe the gospel we preach and victory is ours." I repeat: The reason that a number of us Bible-"toting" and Bible-quoting Christians can't bring forth God's best is that we really don't believe the word that we carry and the words that we speak. The writer hit the nail on the head when he said:

O what peace we often forfeit,
O what needless pain we bear,
All because we do not carry
Everything to God in prayer.

If we intend to bring forth God's best, we *must* believe God's word.

"And she brought forth her first-born son. . . ." Once she was married and was with child, Mary carried herself as such. She couldn't do everything she once did, go every place she once went, or eat or drink everything she once consumed. She had to make certain sacrifices and adjustments in her lifestyle because she was carrying something special within. She was carrying God's best. She was carrying the promise of the ages. She was carrying a special spiritual endowment, and her life had to reflect the same. She had to be consecrated, set apart, and holy to bring forth

God's best. Her whole life revolved around bringing forth that which she carried.

If we would bring forth the best, then we must live as if we are carrying God's best. If we are carrying God's best, then we must live like it. We can't do everything we once did and expect to bring forth God's best. We have to make some sacrifices for the best. Young people, if you would bring forth God's best, then you must be prepared to make some sacrifices. You must be prepared to stay in and study when others go out, or come to church when others do not. You must be prepared to say no when others say yes. When you are accused of being a nerd or a square or stuck up or a Holy Roller, you must tell them that you are not trying to be any of those things. You simply understand that you are carrying something special within you, placed there by God's gracious Spirit, and you are just trying to bring forth the best that is within you.

We can't bring forth the best without sacrifice. If we are athletes, it means going to practice when others go home. If we're Christians, it means going to prayer when others go to the convenient weapons of the world. If we're poor, it means getting our priorities straight and sacrificing for that which is really important. And if we're accused of being cheap, we simply must tell others who don't understand our situation that we are working within the limitations and possibilities that God has placed within us, and that all we're trying to do is bring forth the best.

"And Mary brought forth her first-born son. . . ." In the fullness of time, Mary brought forth. At a time and in a place where she least expected, she brought forth her first-born son. When she received the word of God from the angel, she didn't know the circumstances in which her baby would be born. I'm sure that she didn't expect the birth to occur on a journey. She didn't know that Caesar Augustus would issue a decree stating that the world should be taxed. She didn't know that she and Joseph would have to take a trip to Bethlehem to be enrolled. She didn't know that in distant Bethlehem she would bring forth her firstborn son and wrap him in swaddling clothes and lay him in a manger because there would be no room for them in any of the inns. She didn't know that the first visitors to see her child would not be relatives, but shepherds.

If we believe God's Word and live in such a way that it can be brought to fruition in us, then we will bring forth

God's best. In God's time and in God's way, God's best will come forth. We may not know about the many factors that will coalesce or come together to bring it about, but one thing is certain—if we're faithful, God's best within us will come forth. We may not be able to pick the time or the place, the circumstances, or the people who will be participants, but one thing is certain—it will come. It has to come, because God is behind and in the midst of the process to bring it forth. God planted the seed, and if we have done our part, God will bring it forth.

That's why Habakkuk said: "The vision is yet for an appointed time, but at the end it shall speak, and not lie: though it tarry, wait for it; because it will surely come, it will not tarry" (Habakkuk 2:3, KJV). If we believe the best, live for the best, work for the best, and trust God for the best, then God's best will come forth. As surely as Jesus was born, God's best will come forth. As surely as he arose from the grave after living a life of holiness, God's best will come forth. As surely as Jesus is coming back again with his reward with him, God's best will come forth.

Conclusion:
Let a New Woman Rise

Colossians 3:1–2

William D. Watley

During his lifetime Jesus was called a devil, a blasphemer, a drunkard, a glutton, a friend of tax collectors, and a sinner. And if one reads the Gospels closely, one can also see sufficient evidence for labeling him as a "ladies man." Throughout Jesus' ministry, women were among his most perceptive, most devoted, and most loyal followers. It has been said that in the Gospels, we do not read of a woman being an enemy of Jesus. No woman deserted, denied, betrayed, slandered, or persecuted him. In the last days of Jesus' life, in those closing events of that drama called redemption, consummated at Calvary, women, more than anyone else, seemed to share the suffering of the Master.

On his way to Jerusalem, when he stopped at Bethany, one woman with an alabaster flask of costly ointment poured it on him, and when men criticized her for her extravagance, Jesus defended her and declared that her act of love would be an everlasting memorial unto her, saying: "Let her alone; why do you trouble her? She has performed a good service for me. She has done what she could; she has anointed my body beforehand for its burial. Truly I tell you, wherever the good news is proclaimed in the whole world, what she has done will be told in remembrance of her" (Mark 14:6, 8 – 9, NRSV). When Jesus stood before the governor Pilate, another woman (Pilate's very own wife) was troubled in a dream concerning him. She went to her husband and warned him, "Have nothing to do with that innocent man, for today I have suffered a great deal because of a dream about him" (Matthew 27:19, NRSV). On the way to Calvary, while men were cursing and abusing him, while other men were either scared or ashamed to own him, women courageously and unashamedly followed him and wept. On his way to Calvary he spoke to these women. Not to disciples, the Roman soldiers, or the unruly crowd—he spoke to no one except the women. He tried to comfort and warn only the women. He said, "Daughters of Jerusalem, do not weep for me, but weep for yourselves and for your children" (Luke 23:28, NRSV). While Jesus was dying, women were standing by the cross—not standing in the shadows because of the darkening sky, but standing by the cross; not standing afar in the distance looking on as detached spectators, but standing by the cross. Mary, his mother; his aunt; Mary, the wife of Cleophas; and Mary Magdalene were all standing there. Women were with Christ as he suffered; they were with him to the bitter end.

One wonders why the devotion of women to Christ was and still is so great. I personally don't think it has anything to do with the old chauvinistic and sexist assertion that women are by nature lightheaded, softhearted, and inclined to be romanticists. I think that women were attracted to Jesus for the same reason that men were attracted to him—he was different from any man they had ever met. To begin with, he was a man in the fullest sense of the term. There was nothing weak or immature about him. He was a man when they met him; he wasn't a boy who had to be raised into a man. He was sure of himself, so sure that he wasn't swayed by women's looks or threatened by their intelligence. He didn't need his ego stroked; he did not need to affirm his identity as a male by negating the right of women to have identities of their own as persons; he did not need to oppress and tyrannize women to make himself feel like a man.

Jesus was a man who knew who he was, where he was going, and how to get there; yet he was not so caught up in his own agenda that he couldn't take time out for all people. He was intelligent enough to confound rabbis, but simple enough to be understood by a child. He was great enough to rule the wind and waves, yet humble enough to ride a donkey and wash the feet of his disciples. He was feared by kings, yet loved by common people. He was stern enough to chase moneychangers out of the temple, yet gentle enough to say, "Let the little children come to me, and do not stop them; for it is to such as these that the kingdom of heaven belongs" (Matthew 19:14, NRSV).

Women discovered that not only as a man but also as a teacher and prophet, Jesus was without equal. He never nagged them or flattered them or coaxed them or appealed to their so-called vanity. He rebuked them in love without condescension. He never jeered at them for being female or tried to fit them into his own concept of femininity. He took them as he found them and left them brand new. Most of all, women found that Jesus took them seriously. The pleas of the Syrophoenician woman for her sick child; the plight of the woman caught in the act of adultery; the grief of the widow of Nain who had lost her son; the desperation of the woman with the issue of blood; the questions of the Samaritan woman at Jacob's well; the sacrifices of the widow who gave her two mites; the disappointment of Mary and Martha—all of these were taken seriously by Jesus.

Since Jesus took women seriously, women took him seriously and were willing to go with him, not only to Calvary, but also to the grave. On that third-day morning when Jesus rose, he was greeted, not by the disciples, but by women. According to Matthew's Gospel, Jesus was greeted by Mary Magdalene and the other Mary. According to Mark, it was Mary Magdalene, Mary, the mother of James, and Salome. According to Luke, it was Mary Magdalene, Mary, the mother of James, Joanna, and several others. According to John, it was Mary Magdalene. The Gospel writers may not give the same account as to who was there; however, one thing they are agreed on—Jesus first appeared to women. It was the women who brought to the men the news that Jesus lives and not vice versa. Those who had stood by him to the end, those who had shared in his suffering, those who had claimed him even when he was on the cross, those who had never forsaken him in his life—these were the first to behold him after he had risen. The last became the first to experience the risen Christ in his new glory in his new being with new power.

Therefore, my sisters in the Lord Jesus Christ, I have this challenge for you: If you who have suffered with Christ and have also become part of his resurrection, or (if I may be permitted to slightly alter the text) "If then you have been raised with Christ, then let a new woman rise by seeking the things that are above, where Christ is, seated at the right hand of God. Set your minds on things that are above, not on things that are on earth" (Colossians 3:1 – 2, author's paraphrase).

There is a phrase, popularized in an advertisement directed towards women, that says, "You've come a long way, baby." However, I think that it's rather tragic that this ad, which proclaims the progress of women, is a cigarette ad. While it's true that a double standard (one for men and one for women) in terms of either morality or conduct or pay scales is wrong and that women have a legitimate right to rebel against it, I would also hope and pray that women, especially black women, do not measure their liberation in terms of the privilege and right to participate in the vices of men. It's no great accomplishment to be able to smoke, drink, curse, take drugs, get high, and become as vulgar, profane, and promiscuous as some men. You will only prove that you are equally as foolish, for you will have substituted one oppressor called "man" for another oppressor called "sin." No, if you're going to be truly new, free, and Christian, you can't afford to lower your standards; you must raise them. Mary McLeod Bethune was right: "The true worth of a race must be measured of its womanhood." So then, if you have been raised with Christ, we urge, implore, and beg you, as your men and as your children, to rise above that which is superficial, petty, and mundane and seek those things that are above, where Christ is seated at the right hand of God.

Look how we [men] grovel here below,
Fond of these earthly toys;
Our souls can neither fly nor go
To reach eternal joys.[1]

Look at how we men with our materialistic values work ourselves to death and step on and exploit and oppress others to get those things that do not matter in the long run. We need someone to give us a new outlook, a new "uplook," and new values. We need someone who will help us think new thoughts and new dreams and set on foot a new humanity. We would encourage you that "whatever is true, whatever is honorable, whatever is just, whatever is pure, whatever is pleasing, whatever is commendable, if there is any excellence and if there is anything worthy of praise, think about these things" (Philippians 4:8, NRSV).

All around us we see a new black woman emerging—one that is independent, self-confident, and self-assured;

---

[1]From "Come, Holy Spirit, Heavenly Dove," by Isaac Watts.

one who feels that she doesn't have to take a man's abuse to support either herself or her children; one who believes that before she lowers herself to that, she will shake the dust from her feet and make it on her own. We see an emerging black woman who feels that she doesn't have to live in the shadows of her man, but has a right to her own identity. And although this woman still admires and often desires the roles of mother, wife, and homemaker, she also believes that she doesn't need to feel guilty or less of a woman if she chooses a career that is either independent of or supplementary or complementary to these traditional roles. Black women are saying to us men that they are still willing to go all the way with us as long as we are going to be men, but they don't have a whole lot of either time or patience with our oppression and excuse making. Personally, I'm proud to see black women standing tall, beautiful, with their heads on straight, proud of their blackness and their heritage, refined, and confident. However, I hope that the new black woman, in addition to being beautiful, intelligent, sophisticated, "together," articulate, and refined, is also a godly woman. We don't hear the term "godly woman" too much these days.

We have come as far as we have because black women have been godly women—women who knew the worth of prayer. When men were gone and children were in trouble, they knew how to get down on bended knees and ask God to make a way out of no way. Harriet Tubman was courageous in that she made numerous trips into the deep South to lead blacks to freedom, but she was also a godly woman. Sojourner Truth was noble; she didn't take anything off anybody, but she was also a godly woman. Mary McLeod Bethune was brilliant, but she was also a godly woman. Rosa Parks occupies a key place in the history of the modern civil rights movement, and she is also a godly woman. Read over the list and you will see that those women who have done the most to lift us, no matter what their professions, were also godly women. They knew that whoever the Son sets free—no matter what society or men might say—is free indeed.

If a new black woman is to rise, she must be a combination of the refinement of this present day and the faith of yesterday. If a new black woman is to rise, she must understand that she cannot do it apart from the Christ who gave her the privilege of first beholding him in his resurrection and glory. If a new black woman is to be, she must not only look new and talk new, but she must also be made anew from within. In this day and age with all of its peril and promise, with all of its challenges and opportunities, if a new woman is to emerge, she must be born again. So "if then you have been raised with Christ, seek the things that are above, where Christ is, seated at the right hand of God" (Colossians 3:1 – 2).